WORKS ISSUED
BY THE TEXT AND TRANSLATION SOCIETY

THE SIXTH BOOK

OF THE

SELECT LETTERS OF SEVERUS

PATRIARCH OF ANTIOCH

VOL. II. (TRANSLATION) PART I.

THE SIXTH BOOK

OF THE

SELECT LETTERS OF SEVERUS

PATRIARCH OF ANTIOCH

IN THE SYRIAC VERSION OF ATHANASIUS OF NISIBIS

EDITED AND TRANSLATED

BY

E. W. BROOKS, M.A.

VOL. II. (TRANSLATION) PART I.

PUBLISHED FOR
THE TEXT AND TRANSLATION SOCIETY
BY
WILLIAMS & NORGATE
14 HENRIETTA STREET, COVENT GARDEN, LONDON, W.C.
AND 7 BROAD STREET, OXFORD
1903

INTRODUCTION

Our knowledge of the early life of Severus is mainly drawn from the biography of him by his friend Zacharias the Scholastic of Gaza,[1] existing in a Syriac version published by Dr Spanuth[2] and translated into French by M. Nau.[3] From this we learn that he was a native of Sozopolis in Pisidia and was said to be descended from a Severus who was bishop of that city in 431.[4] Beyond this the life tells us nothing about his family except that he was the third son[5]; but in ep. i. 49 he mentions his brother Peter, a presbyter of Antioch, who was dead when that letter was written.[6] His enemies accused him of having in his youth followed heathen practices,[7] and it was in order to refute this charge that Zacharias wrote his life: but, whether there was any truth in the accusation or not, it must be admitted that the answer is a very lame one. After his father's death he was sent to Alexandria with his elder brothers to study Greek and Latin grammar

---

[1] Used by Evagrius (iii. 33). [2] Göttingen, 1893.

[3] Opuscules Maronites (Rev. de l'Or. Chrét. iv, v).

[4] *Cf.* Land Anec. Syr. i. 14 (113). [5] P. 21 10.

[6] According to the most obvious interpretation of this passage Peter was his brother's *apokrisiarios* at Constantinople.

[7] *Cf.* Mansi viii. 999.

and rhetoric. Thence about 486[1] he proceeded to Berytus to study law with the intention of becoming an advocate; but, while there, he found time for theological reading also, and published his first work, an Encomium of the Apostle Paul. It was not until after this that he was baptized, the ceremony taking place at Tripolis (circ. 488).[2] About 490[3] however, while on a visit to Jerusalem, he came under the influence of the disciples of Peter the Iberian, and became a monk in Peter's monastery between Gaza and Majuma.[4] After a sojourn in the wilderness of Eleutheropolis, where he nearly died from the severity of his ascetic practices, he was entertained and restored to health by the monks of Romanus, returning later to the *laura* of Majuma.[5] Afterwards however he founded a monastery of his own[6] and was ordained presbyter by Epiphanius the confessor.[7] About 508 disturbances were caused in Palestine by a certain Nephalius, who, having been one of the extreme Monophysite party,[8]

[1] Kugener in Rev. de l'Or. Chr. v. 205.

[2] According to Zach. it was said not to be the custom of the Pisidians to baptize infants (p. 2 l. 11).

[3] After the death of Peter the Iberian (Dec. 1, 488): see Kugener in Byz. Zeitschr. ix. 466.

[4] Called by the so-called Zacharias Rhetor (vii. 10) the monastery of Theodore, *i.e.* Peter's successor (vit. Pet. 134, 144; Vailhé in Rev. de l'Or. Chr. v. 45); so 'Dion.' ap. Nau Rev. de l'Or. Chr. ii. 466.

[5] P. 26 l. 4 (*cf.* ep. i. 35). It is not clear whether this was Peter's monastery.

[6] *Cf.* ep. ii. 3 (p. 248 text).

[7] Hardly Epiphanius of Magydum (ep. i. 1), whose date was earlier; but probably the Epiphanius of ep. ii. 3.

[8] *Cf.* Zach. Rh. vi. 2–4.

had turned Chalcedonian, and, probably in conjunction with the patriarch of Jerusalem, expelled many monks from their monasteries. To counteract this movement Severus went to Constantinople, where he wrote a treatise addressed to the patricians Apion and Paul against a charge of Eutychianism, the Philalethes against those who found the Chalcedonian doctrine in Cyril, the Answers to the questions of Eupraxius the chamberlain, and the Refutation of the Testament of Lampetius the Adelphian.[1] Here he remained three years[2] until after the ordination of Timothy to the see of Constantinople (Aug.–Sept. 511); after which he returned to Majuma, and immediately set himself to abolish the Henotikon-compromise, whereby all mention of the Synod of Chalcedon had been avoided, and to procure the deposition of the patriarchs Flavian of Antioch and Elijah of Jerusalem. At the Synod of Sidon Flavian was strongly supported, and the attempt failed; but, further compulsory powers having been obtained from the Emperor, the patriarch was deposed at the Synod of Antioch,[3] and Severus was ordained his successor (Nov. 6, 512),[4] being according to Zacharias accepted by all the bishops of the patriarchate except Epiphanius of Tyre,[5] Flavian's brother, and Julian of Bostra. At this point the work of Zacharias ends, and

---

[1] *Cf.* ep. i. 13. For other works of Sev. see Zach. Rh. vii 10.
[2] P. 29 l. 5.
[3] Zach. Rh. l. c.; Assem. B. O. ii. 18.
[4] Jo. Mal. p. 400; Anec. Syr. i. 14 (113); Evagr. iii. 34.
[5] *Cf.* ep. i. 31.

from the later life by John archimandrite of Kenneshre, the concluding portion of which has been published in a French translation by M. Nau,[1] but scanty information is to be obtained; so that for the events of his patriarchate we have outside the letters little evidence beyond the assertions of his enemies produced at the synod of 536.[2] On the death of Anastasius in July 518 the influence of Vitalian procured from the new Emperor Justin an order for the expulsion of Severus, who on Sept. 29 fled from Antioch,[3] and for the rest of his life lived for the most part in hiding in Egypt, though he continued to be recognised as patriarch by his own party. Here during the earlier part of his exile he wrote the controversial works against Julian the deposed bishop of Halicarnassus, who maintained the incorruptibility of Christ's body.[4] In 531 Justinian recalled the banished monks, and invited the bishops to a conference at Constantinople; but the invitation which he afterwards sent to Severus was declined.[5] In the winter of 534–5, how-

---

[1] Rev. de l'Or. Chr. v. 293 ff. [2] Mansi viii. 979 ff.

[3] Zach. Rh. viii. 2; Anec. Syr. *l.c.*; Mich. Syr. ap. Chabot Rev. de l'Or. Chr. iv. 446. Evagr. (iv. 3) seems to place his flight in 519; and so Theophanes, who gives him 7 years: but the homilies in Brit. Mus. Add. MS. 12,159, which are arranged chronologically, and end with Lent 518, are decisive for the earlier date (Wright C.B.M. 534 ff.); *cf.* also the letter of Dioscorus the deacon in Migne P.L. lxiii. 448. The Copts observe Sept. 29 as the day of his arrival in Egypt (Gutschmid Kleine Schriften, ii. 458).

[4] Add. MS. 17,200; Cod. Syr. Vat. 140; Zach. Rh. ix. 9–13. These works were translated into Syriac in Apr. 528 (Assem. B.O. ii. 46).

[5] Zach. Rh. viii. 5; ix. 15, 16; Evagr. iv. 10, 11; Mansi viii. 817.

ever, the Monophysite tendencies at court having probably under Theodora's influence become more pronounced, he consented to come;[1] and the accession of Anthimus to the see of Constantinople in June 535 seemed to make his position a strong one. But with the arrival of Pope Agapetus came a reaction; and in Mar. 536 Anthimus was deposed, and he and Severus expelled from the city,[2] while at the synod held in May their final condemnation was decreed.[3] On Feb. 8, 538 Severus died in Egypt.[4]

Of the voluminous works of Severus, almost entirely lost in Greek, many exist in Syriac versions, of which not the least interesting are the letters. These letters were divided into three classes, those before episcopacy, those during episcopacy, and those after expulsion, containing 4, 10, and 9 books respectively; besides which there were also letters described as "outside the 23 books."[5] If we take the highest number in each book mentioned in the present collection, and add one for the 6th book of those after expulsion, of which no letters are here preserved, we shall find that the total cannot have been less than 3759. Of these the version of Athanasius comprises 123 only;[6] but, as it is described as the 6th book only of the Select Letters, the whole collection probably

[1] Zach. Rh. ix. 15; Jo. vit. Sev. p. 299; Evagr. iv. 11.
[2] Zach. Rh. ix. 19.
[3] Mansi viii. 874 ff.
[4] Ass. B.O. ii. 54; Anec. Syr. *l.c.*; Mich. ap. Chabot *l.c.*
[5] iv. 7, 10.
[6] Unless there are some lost in sect. x. between B f.144 and A f.99.

contained not less than 700. It is almost certain from the translator's preface that he translated the 6th book only, and that he therefore found the collection existing in Greek and did not make it for himself, as might also be inferred from the fact that it is called by the Greek name ἐκλογαί. This translation was made in the year A.S. 980 (669) by the presbyter Athanasius of Nisibis at the instigation of the bishops Matthew of Berrhœa and Daniel of Edessa,[1] and the letters contained in it are arranged in 11 sections according to subjects, while to each letter a note is appended stating the place which it occupies in the original collection. The order of letters in each section generally, but not always, follows the original order: but on what principle they were primarily arranged it is hard to say; certainly not chronologically, for vi. 178 during episcopacy (v. 5 Ath.) is mentioned in vi. 161 (v. 4) and v. 52 (i. 59) clearly preceded iv. 81 (v. 15), while v. 52 after expulsion (i. 59) preceded iv. 81 (v. 15) and i. 53 or 55 (i. 49) preceded i. 16 (i. 50). In some cases a double reference is given, which may be explained by supposing either that in the original the same letter was sometimes accidentally given twice, or that the order was not the same in all copies.

Besides the version of Athanasius at least two other

[1] A f. 102 ra. Wright (p. 564) would identify the translator with Athanasius Baladaya, afterwards patriarch, who was a Greek scholar (Barh. H.E. i. 287) and translated the *Eisagoge* of Porphyry in 645 (Ass. B.O. i. 493); but this Athanasius was a monk at Kenneshre and Beth Malkhe, not a presbyter of Nisibis.

Syriac versions of the letters were in existence, as we see in the case of v. 6 of our collection, where we find all three versions co-existing; but the other versions survive only in isolated letters and fragments. Both seem to have been in much commoner use than the Athanasian version, and in both, so far as we can judge, the translation was less literal and contained fewer Hellenisms: thus we often find Athanasius giving a Greek word followed by a Syriac interpretation introduced by *aukhith* (or), where the other versions have a Syriac word only.

The letters translated by Athanasius treat only of ecclesiastical matters; but whether the dogmatic letters were excluded from the collection or contained in the other books we have no means of knowing.

In my notes the references to the O.T. are to the LXX (ed. Swete); and the rendering of all Biblical and patristic quotations of which the original exists is made as literal as possible, in order that it may be used as an authority for the text. To avoid misunderstanding, I may explain that in the rendering of theological terms I have invariably translated οὐσία by "essence," *knuma* (ὑπόστασις) by "substance," and πρόσωπον by "person." The practice of using "person" for both the two latter (distinguished by the ancient writers) is indefensible. Questions as to the meaning of rare or difficult words and phrases are reserved for the Vocabulary, which will be given at the end of the text. An index will be appended to the translation of Part II.

E. W. BROOKS.

April 1903.

CONTENTS OF PART I.

PAGE

Introduction v
Syriac translator's Preface and Headings 1

SECTION I.

1 To bp. Constantine 3
2 To Solon bp. of Seleucia in Isauria 12
3 To the same 16
4 To the same 23
5 To Peter bp. of Apamea 34
6 To bp. Nicias 38
7 To Castor bp. of Perga 39
8 To duke Timostratus 41
9 To Stephen bp. of Tripolis 44
10 To bp. Eucharius 46
11 To the archimandrite of the monastery of Bassus 47
12 To Cosmos Polyeuctus and Zeno the presbyters 52
13 To Entrechius bp of Anazarba 53
14 To Antoninus bp. of Berrhoea 57
15 To the same 60
16 To the same 61
17 To Misael the chamberlain 63
18 To Entrechius bp. of Anazarba 66
19 To Solon bp. of Seleucia 67
20 In the name of a synod to the suffragans of Apamea 70
21 To the Master of the Offices 73
22 To the fathers 75
23 To Solon bp. of Seleucia 81
24 To Theotecnus the *archiatros* 83
25 To Dionysius bp. of Tarsus 85
26 To Solon bp. of Seleucia 86
27 To Musonius and Alexander *vindices* of Anazarba 87
28 To Philoxenus bp. of Doliche 89
29 To the monks of the monastery of Isaac 90
30 To the clergy of Apamea 92
31 To the bishops of Phoenice 96

		PAGE
32	To John bp. of Alexandria the less	98
33	To Dionysius bp. of Tarsus	100
34	To the suffragans of Apamea	101
35	To Eustace the presbyter	102
36	To Eusebius deacon of Apamea	103
37	To Simeon bp. of Chalcis	104
38	To the same	106
39	To the clergy and notables of Apamea	110
40	To Hypatius Master of the Soldiers	113
41	To bp. Solon	116
42	To the fathers	119
43	To the archimandrite of the monastery of Simeon	120
44	To Eutychian governor of Apamea	123
45	To Conon the brigand-chaser	125
46	To the clergy of Antaradus	126
47	To Cassian bp. of Bostra	129
48	To Philoxenus bp. of Hierapolis	130
49	To John and John presbyters and archimandrites	132
50	To the same	140
51	To Philip the presbyter	145
52	To John and John the presbyters	148
53	To the Syrian bishops at Alexandria	151
54	(Heading lost)	162
55	To Theodore archimandrite of the monastery of Romanus	164
56	To bp. Proclus	167
57	To bp. Didymus	171
58	To the same	176
59	To Julian archimandrite of the monastery of Bassus	178
60	To Photius and Andrew archimandrites of monasteries in Caria	179
61	(Heading lost)	191
62	(do.)	193
63	To Misael the deacon	195

SECTION II.

1	To the patricians	199
2	To John and John the presbyters	204
3	To the orthodox at Emesa	207

The Sixth Book of the Select Letters of the Holy Severus. p. 1.

He that meets with this book must know that it is not only the topics[1] mentioned in the sectional titles[2] that are included in the letters arranged under these, but that most of them also contain or set forth matter relating to various other subjects. However, they have been arranged under each of the sections[2] in accordance with the larger part of the matter expressed in them.

The sections[2] of the sixth book of the select[3] or chosen letters, taken from the letters of the blessed Severus, patriarch of Antioch in Syria, on doctrines and the words of Scripture.

---

1 κεφάλαια. 2 τίτλοι. 3 ἐκλογαί.

[1.] About [bishops and clergymen and their ordination.

2. About his ordination before episcopacy; and about the precedence of bishops and another doubtful point regarding them; and about men who give themselves out as bishops and ordain; and about the proper ordination of bishops.

p. 2. 3. That one ought not to hesitate on account of the *politeia* or character of priests, but only ask whether they are orthodox or of the right opinions.

4. That one must not communicate indiscriminately or without investigation with heretics; and how one ought to avoid being with them while they pray.

5. About clergymen or laymen] who are converted from heresies.

6. That one must not take account of anathemas or excommunications that are pronounced by heretics.

7. About monks and nuns.

8. About men who cut off their genital members, and about men who have them cut off through necessity, and about men who killed themselves in time of martyrdom, and that it is the custom in many churches for the glories and praises of the saints to be read.

9. About baptisms performed in time of necessity by deacons or by laymen, and about men as to whom there is doubt [whether they have been baptized or not.

10. About a man who has a wife and children and wishes to become a monk: and the same

also about women, and about the marriage of these.

11. That a man who can help or assist the right confession while engaged in state affairs must not become a monk].

The sixth book of the select[1] or chosen letters taken from the letters of the holy Severus, patriarch of Antioch in Syria. p. 3.

I. First section[2]; about bishops and clergymen and their ordination.

---

1. *To Constantine the bishop. (From those before episcopacy, from the 2nd book the 12th letter.)* 508-11.

The contents of your sanctity's former epistle to me are as far from applying to my vileness as the heaven is far from the earth, to use the words of the prophet.[3] For you thought fit to recite to me the passage of the Song of Songs, I mean, "Thou art all fair, my neighbour, and there is no spot [in thee."[4] . . . .]. I [am turned] into another man, as it is written[5] and prophesy, and that not one of all your words shall fall

---

[1] ἐκλογαί.

[2] τίτλος.

[3] Ps. cii. 11.

[4] Ca. iv. 7.

[5] 1 R. x. 6.

to the ground. For he is faithful who said to you high priests, "Ye shall call my name upon the sons of Israel, and I the Lord will hallow them."[1] However, let these things be so. But know, father ours, that, after the holy Asterius the bishop and those with him came here, many various . . . .

. . . .

. . . .

will cast those that are deceived into a pit of destruction. But all, so to speak, have the one object only, to bring to naught the *typos* or formula
p. 4. of satisfaction[2] which seemed good to the pious king, which he also sent to Flavian, the prelate of the city of Antiochus, and either altogether to remove and abolish it, or to cut away some of its exactitude, because they do not intend to drink the still water, as says Ezekiel, but strive to foul it with their own feet,[3] in order that the sheep which have learned to hear the voice of the Good Shepherd, and to drink "the water of Shiloah that goeth softly,"[4] may not be able to avoid the pollution of the drink. Which John of Claudiupolis also tried to do when he came here. When he received me in the house of the glorious Patrick, the Master of the Soldiers,[5] and conversed with me by order of our pious king, he said, "There ought to be introduced into the formula of satisfaction[2]

[1] Nu. vi. 27.
[2] πληροφορία.
[3] Eze. xxxiv. 18.
[4] Is. viii. 6.
[5] στρατηλάτης.

this statement, 'We receive the synod at Chalcedon, not as a definition of faith, but as a rejection of Nestorius and of Eutyches.'[1] Thus both those that are pleased with the Synod will not be angry, and you will receive contentment in that the doctrines which offend you are rejected." But I said, "This argument is silly, and the offspring of a drunken mind. Who is there among right-minded persons who will accept and praise us on account of this disturbance and confusion? If the Synod of Chalcedon introduced the doctrine of Nestorius into the churches, though it called Nestorius 'of small intelligence'[2] in order to entice and deceive those that are more simple, how can we say that it rejected the opinion p. 5.
of Nestorius? But, if the formula of satisfaction[3] in so many words rejects the doctrines of the Synod and of the impious Tome of Leo, which are the life blood of the abomination of Nestorius, how can we honestly say that we accept this synod as against Nestorius? . . . rather we shall be tripped up as by . . ." "What then? Were not those at Chalcedon rightly moved against Eutyches? why, [if] you accept them on this point, do you think them fit . . . an anathema?" [But] I said, "What I am about to say is strange, but nevertheless true. It is especially for this reason that we say that they are men that deserve anathema, because they unnecessarily extended the

[1] *Cf.* Zach. Rh. ix. 20 *ad fin.*; Evag. iii. 31.

[2] Mansi vii. 113.

[3] πληροφορία.

heresy of Eutyches. Owing to the fact that they wished to heal the disorder in an unintelligent way by means of an opposite infection, I mean by the evil impiety of Nestorius, thenceforward those who were infected with the belief in a phantasy, seeing that they were inviting them to man-worship, recoiled from this vicious remedy, and thought themselves all the more pious, and carried their own corruption further. But, if they had been cured and healed by means of right doctrines, they would perhaps have abandoned their
p. 6. infection. [If] we accept those [who] met together [at] Chalcedon as being adversaries [of] the heresy of Eutyches, and praise them on the ground that they spoke well up to a certain point, and do not rather blame them, it is time for us to accept also the Arian heresy, which contends against the evil opinion of Sabellius, and agrees up to a certain point with the right doctrines of the Church, in that it glorifies God the unbegotten Father, and in that it does not confound the three substances, but confines them within their own attributes or persons. But we do not extol it on this account, nor do we judge it to deserve a partial anathema. But, because it calls the Son and the Holy Spirit creatures, and degrades them to a servile position, on this account it is utterly repudiated by the orthodox doctors of the Church. This same trick we find practised by the other heresies also. By displaying a certain part of the sound faith as a decoy and mixing[1] with this the vanity of their

[1] This is the meaning needed, though I cannot supply the word.

own profane words they thus appear plausible to those that are more innocent and simple; but we do not, on account of the sound part, hold back and shrink from repudiating them, but we anathematize them with all our power." When the good and excellent John had heard these things, he betook himself to another topic.[1] He asked me p. 7.
whether Epiphanius the bishop,[2] who is among the saints, performed our ordinations fitly and in accordance with the canon. But I said, "Very well and most properly," and "after the pattern of the doctors and stablishers of the word of the orthodox faith. For he in his boyhood was brought up in monasteries, and practised a virginity modelled on the angelic and unembodied life, being a citizen of Perga: a man of no ignoble city, as it is written,[3] yes, and a man of noble birth also, if these things are not small to the citizens of Jerusalem above. Having been advanced to the bishopric of Magydum (this also is a city in Pamphylia) at the time of the Encyclical which repudiated the impiety that was confirmed at Chalcedon, under which Timothy, who was sent into exile for piety's sake, returned to Alexander's city, and received back the presidency of the flock of Mark the Evangelist, which before was unrighteously tended by wolves and torn, when he saw that the bishops had changed, and that they had overthrown the Encyclical by a contrary

[1] κεφάλαιον.

[2] *Cf.* Zach. Rh. v. 5.

[3] Ac. xxi. 39.

document, and had gone back to the Synod of Chalcedon and its hateful doctrines, he left his throne and
p. 8. Pamphylia, the land of his fathers, and the blessed man came as a fugitive to Alexander's city, and embraced communion with the saintly Timothy, the champion of the right faith, having taken joyfully upon him the spoiling of his goods, and knowing that he had in heaven a better and enduring inheritance, as the wise Paul says.[1] But, when Timothy of holy memory had finished his course and kept his faith[2] and departed to God, the zealots of the orthodox faith were again persecuted in Alexander's city, and the correct word was perturbed by certain men's mixture. Then therefore the blessed Epiphanius withdrew to Palestine, the stranger on the earth, who did not know any city of his own, or rather knew that only as his own in which God over all is purely worshipped. And, having associated with Peter of Iberia of holy memory, the God-clad man, who was bishop of one of the cities in Palestine, and with the other holy fathers and orthodox peoples, he was persuaded by them and ordained priests, not going beyond the meaning of the sacred canons (far be it!) The canon that forbids a bishop to perform an ordination in provinces[3] or parishes which do not belong to him[4] comes into play
p. 9. in cases where he forces himself upon other men's countries in a disorderly fashion and without an invita-

[1] He. x. 34.
[2] 2 Ti. iv. 7.
[3] ἐπαρχίας.
[4] Mansi ii. 1313, 1317.

tion from anyone, not when he is persuaded to ordain by the bishop of the country or city and by the orthodox clergymen, especially in time of persecution. We may find such instances also if we study church histories. In the times of the Arians, when the servants of piety were persecuted and suffered every kind of evil, Eusebius the bishop of Samosata (this is one of the cities of Mesopotamia) went about the cities and deserts and villages, and travelled to countries outside the boundaries, wearing a soldier's dress and having his head covered by a hood, and applied his sacred hand and confirmed priests for places that were in need; who also put on a crown of martyrdom, having his head crushed by a stone by the heterodox, and migrated in saintly fashion to Jesus who longed for him, and was admitted to the heavenly mansions. These things are clearly stated by Theodoret in his church history.[1] The great light of the Cappadocians also, or rather of the whole world, Basil the bishop, the pillar of the church, the 'sure foundation'[2] (for these words of the apostle fit him more than any man, as fine raiment a bride), was raised to the throne of the bishopric, receiving ordination to the episcopacy, by bishops outside the boundaries. This Gregory the Theologian p. 10.
says in the funeral discourse on Basil himself, writing thus: 'He is raised to the high throne of the bishopric, not without toil nor without envy and contention on

[1] Theod. H.E. v. 4. [2] 2 Ti. ii. 19.

the part of the prelates of the country, and of the worst men of the city who ranged themselves with these; however, the Holy Spirit was bound to conquer: yes, and it does conquer, gaining an easy victory. For from outside the boundaries it stirs up men to anoint, men distinguished and zealous in the matter of piety.'[1] But, if Basil, the teacher of orthodoxy and rule and law of all church discipline, was anointed and received ordination (for this is the anointing of a high-priest) from those outside the boundaries, because the people of the country or province[2] were jealous of him, on account of the Arian heresy or for other human reasons, which is a very small thing, how can we say that the ordinations that were performed among us by a man outside the boundaries, when the transgression of Chalcedon and the Nestorian heresy bare rule and prevailed, are not to be approved? and we have such great and wonderful instances of holy men and such as these, whose zeal is resembled by ours. But what shall we for our part say of the ordinations that are now performed in the churches? What canon re-
p. 11. specting these is not trampled upon? Are not high-priesthoods now everywhere for sale, as we see in the case of civil governorship of cities (the other things I pass over, lest by falling into evil speaking or back-biting and saying things suited to other men I be thought to be choosing for myself matters that do not concern me)?" While I was saying these things, the

[1] Or. xliii. 37.

[2] ἐπαρχία.

gentle John covered his face. But since perhaps, even after he has returned to you, he will again circulate the same suggestions (for this is the habit of those who cause confusion), I have thought it right to make known to your sanctity the details of our honest and lawful discussion of this matter in this royal city. As to the state of our affairs, I think the religious presbyter Peter has once already given you information by letter upon each several point. Still it is a matter for your saintly prayers that the Lord, as is said in the Psalms, after we have "passed through fire and water" may "bring us out into a place of refreshment."[1] But you as watchful shepherds and strict disciples of the chief shepherd Jesus, who brought us up with Him from among the dead by the blood of the everlasting covenant, "stand fast in the faith, quit you like men, and be strong. Let all your things be done with"[2] orthodoxy or the right opinions. For you have "chosen the good part, which shall not be taken away p. 12.
from"[3] you. And we believe that the whole lump also will coalesce with your holy first fruit[4] and be kneaded: for through your prayers we have in all our troubles gained experience of the help of God, and the comfort of hopes of success has not departed from us. *The end.*

Letters like this, of the same tenour, were written to the patricians also, and to Œcumenius.

[1] Ps. lxv. 12.
[2] 1 Co. xvi. 13.
[3] Lu. x. 42.
[4] Ro. xi. 16.

508-11. 2. *Of the same to Solon, bishop and metropolitan.* (*From those before episcopacy, from the 4th book the* 105*th*, 106*th letter.*)

If anyone who knows how to discern spiritually the dispensations of the Lord, who does all things with wisdom, will recall to mind your struggles on behalf of the orthodox faith,—*And after other things.* Henceforth clothe yourself in the immaterial dress of the priesthood, and stand firm. Instead of the ephod take upon your shoulders the Lord's cross; and instead of the tunic woven of fine linen and blue stuff put on the many-coloured tunic of virtues; and strengthen yourself by the struggles of the martyrs which extended
p. 13. to blood. But assuredly the honourable in virginity and first of female martyrs, and skilled maker of these things, I mean the holy Thecla, will clothe you in such raiment to do honour to her vote concerning you. But the crown of the orthodox faith, and purity and good character, and sincerity and vehemence of preaching, by which others also will be stirred up to the same zeal, will be to you the mitre and the crown of gold and the fair-sounding bells. And you are girt with a girdle and a breastpiece, a solitary and unwedded walk in life. Wherefore also Christ shall lie upon your breast, the Word of God, who took flesh for us, who was typified beforehand by the robe and knowledge and truth.[1] When therefore things are thus

[1] Ex. xxviii. 4–35; Le. viii. 7–9.

with you, who will dare to find fault with the innovation in the matter of your institution, when so many bishops with one accord canonically performed the ordination? That a patriarch or a metropolitan or the synod of the province[1] should according to custom ordain such and such a man is not a matter of the strictness of the canons, but rather of church discipline. But this discipline we see to have been often neglected in times of persecution. Take the holy Basil. Because the bishops of the province[1] were adversely disposed towards him, partly from envy, partly because they were attached to the madness of Arius, Gregory p. 14.
the Theologian says that he was ordained by bishops outside the boundaries, writing thus in the funeral discourse on him: [Here follows the citation given above, p. 9]. However, Flavian may be caught by his own wings. If he himself, and that when accused of heresy, formerly ordained someone in Germanicupolis, and snatched away an ordination that belonged to the metropolitan, let him not be annoyed when he has been treated in the same way, when on our side we have an advocate in defence of a similar act in the orthodox faith; and what can a man think could be a better advocate than this? This has the approval of the holy Gregory the Theologian also when he writes in this manner in the first of the conciliatory discourses, I mean that on the union of the monks, when certain men, perhaps like these, were thought to have intro-

[1] ἐπαρχία.

duced an innovation contrary to the law of the Church: "For for our part we received the heads also who were given to the severed part with joy, inasmuch as they introduced an innovation on behalf of piety and to help the right teaching which was in distress, and we did not turn away our faces as from enemies, but welcomed them as our brothers, who for a short time were at discord respecting the paternal inheritance, in a brotherly but not a wicked manner. And we did not praise them on account of the enmity: but we received them on account of the zeal. For separation for piety's
p. 15. sake is better than vicious concord. And for this reason we made the loss our gain, silently removing by love the supposition that there was against us: and to this extent we changed the order of things, that the gift should not follow the election, but the election the gift; and we made use of other men's hands in this matter, having been a little anticipated by the Spirit."[1] From the citation it is possible to discern clearly that the innovation which was thought to have been introduced at that time was one similar to the present position, and that, while the election and the right of ordaining belonged to one set of men, others ordained, especially from his expression, "and we made use of other men's hands in this matter"; and above again, "who for a short time were at discord respecting the paternal inheritance." But he shows that those who had the right to elect and ordain, one among whom in

[1] Or. vi. 11.

particular was the holy Gregory himself, concurred in the election with those who on account of zeal for the orthodox faith had once made an innovation, by uniting with those who separated and made the innovation, and accepting what had been done by them, in that they said, "and for this reason we made the loss our gain, silently removing by love the supposition that there was against us; and to this extent we changed the order of things, that the gift should not follow the election, but the election the gift."

If Gregory the Theologian, and that being orthodox, p 16.
or rather a guide and teacher of orthodoxy, bore with and endured those who seceded from him out of superfluous zeal, and accepted the things done by them by way of innovation, let Flavian, who is infected with heresy, either change his evil belief under teaching, and rejoice with us in the things done by us; or if he remains such as he is let him justly suffer annoyance, and put up with it, enwrapped as he is in the bonds of impiety. But, since there was also contained in your letter the question on what conditions it is right to adopt a union with those of the same opinions, it is necessary to say this much. It is right to unite with those of the same opinions, when they are of the same opinions in everything. Putting aside the complete union of the holy churches, since that needs a lawful concession on certain points, the man who privately wishes to be united with you must in everything seek the same ends; as Constantine also of God-loving memory proclaimed to the people before the church;

the mention of the Henotikon only being passed over as superfluous: for, if it does not touch the stumbling-blocks that sprang up at Chalcedon and separated the churches, what is the use of mentioning it? To the pious king this was necessary for the general union of the churches, since he was desirous of showing that the
p. 17. king who preceded him also had before him the object of bringing into union those who separated on account of the synod at Chalcedon, and that he is not now the first to introduce this question into the churches, as if making an innovation. We for our part therefore have written these things out of our poverty, because you bade us do this also, giving us an example of a modest or humble disposition. But you will of yourself add things greater and better than these, inasmuch as you have already received from the Spirit together with the pastorate ability also to feed the flock with understanding. *The end.*

518-7. 3. *Of the same to the same Solon, bishop and metropolitan of Seleucia in Isauria. (From those during episcopacy, from the 2nd book the 24th letter.)*

The letter of your religiousness was enough to bring even those who are not easily roused to wrath into a state of anger and indignation. But for our part, because we are accustomed to endure such things
p. 18. philosophically, especially when they are done and

said by honoured and beloved men like you, we have thought it right in this instance also not to strive with contentious words, but rather, as far as possible, in consonance with the actual truth to write such things as are in accord with the judgments of God, and to show that we are free from all cause of blame on your part. Callistus was not dragged before us by anyone upon any new charges being made against him by you. Then he would have had ground for complaint, inasmuch as discipline would, as you say, have been violated, and a judgment and cause[1] that belonged to the holy throne of the metropolitan would have been forcibly removed before examination or pardon by being called up, as one may say, to the exaltation and height of the patriarchal and apostolic throne. But, if the matters upon which the party of Hilarian and Musonius made charges against Callistus were examined and investigated while your holiness was in this great city, how comes it that the transaction does not lie beyond the reach of your objections? Nay, how can you avoid praising us if you again recall to your memory how I turned benevolent ears to such faults, and to the bitter attacks of the accusers, and that with much p. 19.
wise moderation we tempered the vehemence of those men, and the gravity of the accusations in which he was involved; and that after this we further in some sort sent a request, which otherwise would not have beseemed us, to each of the bishops, asking them,

[1] ὑπόθεσις.

inasmuch as he had repented, to vote unanimously for the forgiveness which was to be granted him; and, upon our showing such solicitude, he received letters from each of the bishops, and we received these with joy, and immediately the things written were read, and the decree of pardon followed? But, as for the matter which is now thought by Hilarian to be connected with the same subject,[1] how will it be suited for the hearing of your love of God, and that when the sin was directed against me, I mean that of the forged letter? For I do not know if anyone else among men, or an angel from heaven, will come and disprove its spuriousness, seeing that its prejudice is so manifest, and that Hilarian's handwriting also, when compared with his other signatures, utters, so to speak, a voice and proclaims the fiction. Therefore look into these things with carefulness and sincere God-loving thought, and
p. 20. consider whether you are not making a preposterous request, viz., that the patriarch should receive judgment from your love of God in a case of insults or sins that were directed against him, and that in the words sung by everyone you may turn things upside down; and whether we ourselves have not now the right to use your words, "I am insulted and contemned." I forbear to mention that, even after the conviction from the letter, Paul, the God-loving bishop of the city of the Olbians, came here, and bore witness and said that Hilarian said in the presence of his love of God that

[1] ὑπόθεσις.

with Musonius' assent he wrote that the diaconate ought to be restored to Callistus, but that he should not in addition be archdeacon also, and hold the first place.[1] But what is the modest defence to these things, which is given even by your sanctity (for this is the wonderful thing)? "Callistus is not subject to reproof for saying of himself that he does not communicate with us in the matter of the mention of Peter and Palladius, who are by a violation of strict accuracy named in the sacred tablets, and in the matter of communion with the God-loving bishop of the city of the Hierapolitans, Philoxenus, who names a man who signed the things unlawfully done at Chalcedon." May the all-holy soul of Constantine hear these words, against whom that wicked man p. 21.
armed himself, both by writing to those on the other side and by creeping into the archive-house, and arming and inciting the governor[2] of the province[3] to do everything that could bow down his venerable old age and subvert the orthodox faith! For so much did he infuriate him, I mean the governor of Isauria at that time, that death alone put a stop to his fury against piety. May Solon also, who succeeded to Constantine's see, hear these words! and let him hold Callistus as a teacher of zeal for strict accuracy, because after intolerable impieties he has of his own accord come forth as an unlawful champion on behalf of the laws of the church, one who sprang suddenly from the ground

[1] *Cf.* p. 31. [2] ἡγμών. [3] ἐπαρχία.

like the giants fabled in legends. However let Callistus stand upon this peak, there is no objection, and let Solon go up with him. Only let them stay in this citadel, and not immediately come down and say, "All the cities of Isauria have also introduced into the sacred tablets the names of those who unlawfully signed at Chalcedon"; for it is time for me also to say what the well-disposed robber, who was crucified with our Lord and Saviour Christ, said to the blasphemous
p. 22. robber, "Dost not even thou fear God, seeing thou art in the same judgment?"[1] These things we for our part say out of an abundant choice. But anyone who makes a careful investigation will find that your love of God has not maintained the order of things[2] which you took over from Constantine the metropolitan who is among the saints, but that your feathers have gradually fallen off after the manner of a bird, while our meanness has carried out a gradual progress, and has in no way fallen short of the beginning previously made. Indeed every one of those who were ordained by us, whether he incurred dangers or was free from danger, removed the names under suspicion. For neither is the statement made by your religiousness true, I mean that the God-loving Mammian bishop of the city of the Damascenes mentions the name of one who signed. Immediately upon his setting foot in the city and sacrificing the first sacrifice and at the same time with it he offered to God the legal omission of his

[1] Lu. xxiii. 40.

[2] καταστασις.

name. But the omission of the mention of such men as Peter and Palladius we for our part have for the present not promised to any man. The things that must be yielded to junctions or general unions of God's holy churches are both regulated and defined, and we p. 23.
never stretch ourselves to things outside the bounds of moderation, "being vainly puffed up,"[1] as the apostle says, and wandering outside the royal road. If we had in the beginning yielded this difficulty in these other names to you who did this, but had stopped at this one only, that of those who signed as you say several times, how could I on my own authority have laid either upon myself or upon those who have in no way attained to this strictness "heavy burdens and grievous to be borne,"[2] according to the Gospel saying, which injure the right teaching of the faith and upset everything owing to the stress and difficulty of the present time? The things done in the case of Callistus are therefore as stated above. But your love of God ought also to reflect upon the accusations that Musonius and Hilarian brought in the case of the devout Eustace, and how we for our part dealt with the affair in a proper way and in a seemly fashion; and to see with your eyes how honourable is the place that you hold before us, though you show an appearance of forgetting. Indeed I know clearly that in the matters in which it is my duty to trouble my mind I have not relaxed at all. But, if any man seeks to be burdened

[1] Col. ii. 18. [2] Mt. xxiii. 4.

by God's laws, "we have no such custom, neither the
p. 24. churches of God."[1] But may the Lord be witness for me of my words and of the feelings of my heart, that I am still even now praying that Callistus may be found upon manifest proofs to be innocent of the charges made against him, as the previous proceedings also and the various measures taken by me in his case showed! But, if he shall neglect the right road of defence and take refuge in an accuracy of names that does not exist, and in the fact that he does not communicate with us, it is time for me to say to him appropriately the words of Jeremiah, "'If thou whiten thyself with natron and take thee much soap, thy sins have scarred thee before me' saith the Lord."[2] But neither will the religious Hilarian escape from the strict execution of the canons, if he be proved to be lying. A certain term of days has been fixed for him, and this has been set down in writing; and, if he fail to appear and make no defence to the accusation against him, Callistus will be released from the interdict, and the position of a man under a charge will rightly pass to him, as disturbing the discipline of the Church. *And after other things.* But you must believe that, after I had given the letter to the devout Stephen, something that had been omitted came into my mind, I mean, to tell you the time within which the religious bishop Hilarian is to come, or else the things stated in the letter about Callistus and about him will be carried

[1] 1 Co. xi. 16.

[2] Jer. ii. 22.

out. The time is reckoned from to-day, and extends p. 25.
to the end of the month of September. *The end.*

4. *Of the same to the same Solon the bishop.* (*From* 516–17.
those during episcopacy, from the 2nd book the 42nd, 50th letter.)

That there are limits even to long-suffering the sacred scripture clearly teaches us, in that it speaks thus in the person of God over all, "All the day I have spread out my hands unto a gainsaying and disobedient people":[1] and again: "Thus saith the Lord, 'Have I become a wilderness to them of the house of Israel, or a desert land? Because my people said, "We will not be brought into subjection, and we will come no more unto thee."'"[2] What therefore is one to say about Musonius, who was known to us for impudence and rustic denseness, and for love of money which is greater than all evil things, which Paul who had Christ speaking in him said is "the root of all evil?"[3] Being excited by these same passions, he did not notice that he was blinded by beams and searching for other men's motes through love of fault-finding and not in order to guard the salvation of the brethren; insomuch as to upset the whole province[4] as far as his power extends, disturbing both bishops and laity, and
on his own authority adding burdens to burdens, and p. 26.

[1] Is. lxv. 2; Ro. x. 21.
[2] Jer. ii. 31.
[3] 1 Ti. vi. 10.
[4] ἐπαρχία.

not allowing them to arrive at excellence by gradual advance, but by his arrogance to cause those who were standing rightly to go over to the adversaries: insomuch that yet another prophecy is adapted for quoting against him which says, "My sheep fed upon the trampling of your feet, and drank the water that was fouled by your feet; and ye thrust them with your sides and with your shoulders, and ye pushed them with your horns; everyone that was sick ye oppressed, till ye had driven them out, and my sheep were scattered upon every crossway";[1] and again, "That which was weak ye did not strengthen, and that which was sick ye did not heal, and that which was broken ye did not bind up, and that which was in evil plight ye did not comfort, and that which was wandering ye did not bring again, and that which was lost ye did not seek, and that which was sound ye subjected by force."[2] Of all these things he has been guilty, and as far as in him lies he has made havoc of the province.[3] To the orthodox he is burdensome and hostile, and is always kicking his neighbours and pushing them with his horns and gnashing his teeth, like unbroken asses or bulls or wild boars which feed in bestial fashion; but against the adversaries he has never dared to speak so much as a word, but sits inside his house and lives in fear; for such is the boldness which in face of those against whom it is right to be
p. 27. bold shrinks and draws back, but in committing illegal

[1] Eze. xxxiv. 19, 21. [2] *Ibid.* 4. [3] ἐπαρχία.

deeds is precipitous and easily moved to action, and turns everything upside down. Finally, saying that he had become a man according to the saying of the prophet,[1] because he loved strange men and went after them, he went away and found those who could satisfy his avarice and fill his hand. And he did not even think it wrong to exact interest: but, when the God-loving bishops were assembled here, he piteously alleged poverty and want, and openly confessed that for this reason he followed the avaricious practice of taking interest. And, though we gave him many admonitions, he did not even promise to withhold his hand from the unconsecrated means of gain for the future, and that though we ourselves gave him twelve gold pieces and promised to pay him that sum every year, and to relieve the needs of the church that had been entrusted to him; for this he used, so to speak, to bewail every day, going so far as to speak to one of our religious presbyters, whose name is Hesychius, in so many words thus, with the rusticity that is natural to him, "By God! what do you care, you who receive the stipend[2] of the clergy of Antioch, while I possess nothing in my city, not so much as six *denarii*?" When I wrote to you before also, I quoted in the letter his abominable, unholy words, full of sacrilege, which p. 28.
he dared to write in an epistle to our religious presbyter Longinus; and they also are word for word as follows:[3]—"But you remember that I said to you,

[1] Job xxxiii. 25 (?). [2] διάρια. [3] *Cf.* p. 80.

'He ought to have sent something to our church as treasures.[1] By this means not only do the men themselves become more enthusiastic, but the other cities also which are in error, as if they were jealous of us, would have come over and entered into accord with us. In this way Flavian also acted to the bishop of Germanicupolis, when he gave both robes and treasures[1] to the unholy Bisula, and he drew the inhabitants of his country to him.' And your holiness also reported these words to the same holy patriarch, and you told me that you told him and he did not help you at all." What are we to say of a man who from such passions left his flock and would not submit to be poor with Christ, who, while as God He was rich, became poor of His own accord for our sake? This I say, because the money-lover called moderate means poverty, and because, now that he has reached this incurable depth of wickedness, it is absolutely necessary to strip him of the priestly functions, and to subject him to the punishment prescribed by the holy canons.[2] For
p. 29. the seventeenth canon runs thus:—"Since many, while enrolled in the canon, by pursuing after covetousness and base gains have forgotten the divine text that says, 'He hath not put out his money upon interest,' and exact *hekatostai* or one per cent. when they lend, the holy synod has decided, that, if after this ordinance anyone be found receiving interest, contriving the matter by commerce or otherwise, and

[1] κειμήλια.

[2] *Cf.* i. 23.

exacting *hemioliai* or half the whole, or contriving anything else for the sake of filthy lucre, his deposition from the clergy shall follow, and that he shall be an alien to the canon."[1] The hundred and seventh law also, laying down the same principles, says plainly as follows:—"Priests must not lend and receive interest, and what are called *hemioliai*."[2]

But as to Paul, who I would had never become bishop of the city of the Olbians, who because of a provocation that deserves to be treated with contempt left his flock, and was often admonished by me and calmed his savageness, and said that he would be calm and remain at peace and stay in his church, and "returned again to his vomit,"[3] it is necessary for us to use the prophetic words and say, "We healed Babylon, and she was not healed. Let us leave her."[4] Having p. 30.
a dispute with the religious Hilarian, bishop of Diocæsarea, about a certain monastery,[5] an unhallowed and unseemly dispute, but still a dispute, he closed his ears to the apostolic statutes, and would not give them any admission, the statutes that say, "Behold! already ye are utterly in fault that ye go to law with one another; why do ye not rather take wrong? why do ye not rather suffer yourselves to be defrauded? but ye wrong and defraud and that your brethren; or know ye not that unrighteous persons shall not inherit the kingdom of God?"[6]; and often, when he argued in a childish and rustic manner about this, I persuaded

[1] Mansi ii. 676. [2] *Ibid.* 563. [3] Pr. xxvi. 11.
[4] Jer. xxviii. 9. [5] *Cf.* pp. 69, 86. [6] 1 Co. vi. 7–9.

him and restored him to a proper state of mind. For he used always to swear and say that he had great faith in me, and that he revered my labours and struggles on behalf of the orthodox faith (I am even compelled to become a fool[1] by quoting words in my own praise in order to show his disposition). And he would depart from our presence, as if he had been delivered from thoughts that wallow on the earth. But, being bound up in earthly things and infected with the perversity of strife, he would again abandon him-
p. 31. self to the same contentiousness. And, being wholly swayed by anger, and swelling with contentious strifes, he would at one time go up to the royal city, and at another hasten to other countries. And at last, out of love of base gains, he went over to the schism of Musonius, the same Musonius who in his letter to the religious presbyter Longinus, which I mentioned a short time ago, with regard to the same Paul made, sentence for sentence and word for word, such statements as these: "But I will make yet another small addition to the letter. In everything I blame myself. I caused him to be made bishop of Olba, because I thought that there was some good in him, since he displayed an appearance of undergoing a struggle for the faith. And it turned out contrary to my expectations. For he had a mad and wicked strife about a place which was subject to pay tribute to the lord Hilarian the bishop, while he wished to make this

[1] 2 Co. xii. 11.

subject to himself; and the afore-mentioned saintly bishop Hilarian bore with him as long as possible, but, not finding in him any advance towards settling the affair,[1] at last appropriated the place to himself by setting up an altar there. For it was a monastery. But Paul p. 32.
went out of his mind and became like a demon and wrought every kind of disorder, reviling me also. He says he will come there to you. If this happens, write to me and I will come with the lord Hilarian also, and expose all his conduct. God forgive me and be merciful to me! he is not worthy to set foot even on the doorway of the church owing to the deeds done by him. I tremble and am afraid to repeat in the letter the facts regarding him, lest I pollute your ears which are benevolent and God-loving. May the holy God himself grant your holiness to me! For you are always our refreshment and consolation, whenever we remember your name." What mercy therefore can one admit in the case of men who are so foolish, and have unreasonably abandoned their flock on account of base and unhallowed passions, while the sacred canons do not give them any forgiveness, but the eighty-first canon plainly says: "If any presbyter or deacon or generally anyone of the sacred order should leave his own parish and pass to another, and afterwards, completely removing, try to live in another parish for a long time, he shall not minister any more; and especially if when his own bishop calls him and

[1] κατάστασις.

admonishes him to return to his own parish he should
p. 33. not obey; and, if he should continue in the same dis-
orderly conduct, his complete deposition from the
ministry shall follow, so that he shall not again have a
chance of returning to his place; but, if when his
deposition takes place for this reason, another bishop
should receive him, he also shall receive punishment
from a general synod, as breaking the church laws."[1]
And moreover the purport of the eighty-seventh
canon also is the same, and it says thus: "The
bishops in each of the provinces must know that
the bishop who stands at their head in the metro-
polis is himself entrusted with the care of the whole
province, because those who have business meet in the
metropolis from every place; wherefore it has seemed
good that he shall also be the first in honour, and the
other bishops shall do nothing outside the ordinary
course without him, in accordance with the canon that
has prevailed from the beginning from the time of the
fathers, but only those things which belong to each
man's province[2] and to the districts under this; for
each of the bishops has authority to administer his own
parish, in proportion to the devoutness that has fallen
to the lot of each, and to undertake the care of all the
district that is under his city, in so far as to ordain
presbyters and deacons, and to administer each matter
p. 34. with judgment or examination, but not to do anything
outside the course, or even try to do so, without the

[1] Mansi ii. 1309.

[2] ἐπαρχία (Gk. παροικία).

bishop of the metropolis. Neither shall he again do this without the consent of the other bishops."[1] It is a long task to quote the things that are laid down in various places by the holy canons. However it is manifest from the citations made that, since Musonius and Paul have offended against the intention of all church discipline by leaving their country, they have made themselves aliens to the high-priestly office, since they have run counter to Him who said, "The good shepherd layeth down his life for his sheep: but he that is an hireling and is not the shepherd, and whose own the sheep are not, when he hath seen the wolf coming, leaveth the sheep and fleeth, and the wolf seizeth and scattereth them: but the hireling fleeth because he is an hireling, and careth not for the sheep."[2] I had nearly omitted yet another fact which also affords a manifest proof of the madness and of the foolish impulses of Musonius. When he was making a charge against the devout archdeacon Callistus on the ground that he had bought the priestly order and status, thereby satisfying his wrathful inclination, and not actuated in any way by religious motives, he wrote to us to the effect that such a man as that ought to retire from the archidiaconate, but minister in the order of deacons.[3] And he heard me quote, and with p. 35.
great justice, the passage of holy scripture that says, "May thine own mouth convict thee and not I!",[4] and that also which was spoken by the divine Daniel to the

[1] Mansi ii. 1311. [2] John x. 11–13. [3] *Cf.* p. 19. [4] Job xv. 6.

presumptuous elders, on one occasion, "Rightly hast thou also lied against thine head," and on another, "O thou that hast grown old in evil days, now have thy sins come near which thou usedst to commit aforetime, in judging unjust judgments, and in condemning the innocent, and in acquitting the guilty, when the Lord saith, 'The innocent and righteous thou shalt not slay.'"[1] "For, if, as you say, he bought for money the grace that may not be bought, such a man ought to be removed not only from the archidiaconate, but also from the diaconate itself." What then is his ignorant and very rustic defence to this? "Callistus, while archdeacon, puts a stumbling-block in the others' way by carrying the holy gospel on his breast." "What does he[2] say then, madman, to the ignorant person who is near him? Do you think that the cup of salvation of the divine blood has less virtue than the book of the holy gospels, and that the onlookers will not strike upon a greater stumbling-block, when a man who has bought the ministry carries this?" It seems to me that I am doing a superfluous thing in insisting on speaking words without eloquence to men who have contracted this unholy infection. These words your
p. 36. sanctity ought to speak to those who have remained sound, and to call to you the saintly bishops of your province,[3] who confess the orthodox faith, and hold the same communion with us, but strip those men of the priesthood, inasmuch as they did not spare the rational

[1] Su. 59, 52, 53. [2] A 'What shall I.' [3] ἐπαρχία.

sheep, but reckoned the salvation of these secondary to their own passions, and left these as in a night in which is no brightness, and tried to submerge them so deeply in the turbid drink that they should not even have power to rise. However we believe that they will find such efforts vain. For by the mandate of the divine Spirit, and the lawful vote of the citizens through the mediation of your sancity, bishops and high-priest will be ordained for the cities who will feed their flocks with understanding. For he that speaks through Ezekiel says, "Behold! I will seek out my sheep, and will visit them. As the shepherd visiteth his flock on a day of storm and darkness when his sheep are scattered, so will I seek my sheep, and I will deliver them from every place wherein they have been scattered on the day of storm and darkness."[1] Therefore visit these sheep with the help of God, and do not show negligence or give any occasion for delay, lest you bring yourself under the condemnation of these men, and draw upon your head the sentence hanging over them. For we may hear yet another sacred utterance p. 37.
of the prophet which says, "Cursed is he that shall do the works of the Lord negligently, and cursed is he that shall keep back his sword from blood."[2] As there is a time for mercy, so also there is a time for cutting off: for we hear the same Spirit saying in Koheleth, "There is a time to plant, and a time to pluck up that which is planted: a time to kill, and a time to heal: a

[1] Eze. xxxiv. 11, 12.

[2] Jer. xxxi. 10.

time to break down and a time to build,"[1] and the other passages through which we understand how that it is with judgment that we must handle the divine words and fulfil the ministry of these. *The end.*

514–8. 5. *Of the same to Peter, bishop of Apamea. (From those during episcopacy, from the 3rd book the 5th letter.)*

When the letters of your love of God came before me, not that only which was written to me, but that also which was written to the religious presbyter Thomas, I thought it right not to judge words which were put forward, as you yourself also say, under a feeling of wrath and anger, but only to declare my mind as if God himself were listening, and to say to Him like Jeremiah, "The things which came forth from my lips are before Thy face."[2] In the first
p. 38. place you bring a charge against us, which is not known to the canons, nor to the church laws or precepts. For what law of the God-inspired scripture, or precept of the holy fathers, encloses and confines the laity in cities and in countries, and prevents these from going to receive ordination from anyone willing to give it? And how is it that this new charge, which has hitherto escaped the notice of many, has found such a strict prosecutor in you alone? It

[1] Ec. iii. 2, 3.

[2] Jer. xvii. 16.

is time for the God-loving bishop Julian of the city of the Emesenes also to make the same accusation against us in the case of the devout deacon Irenæus, because he registers his fathers' house at Emesa. The saintly Dionysius also, who has reached extreme old age, and is crowned with honourable white hairs, who is venerable for the length of his life, will perhaps more justly put forth a complaint against us, in the case of the religious deacon Anatolius. For in fact he too was previously thought to be a citizen of the city of the Tarsians. And I am sure that the purpose which we had as to the magnificent count Œcumenius is also not unknown to you. Have I therefore up to this day been interfering with all these shepherds of metropolitan sees and causing them annoyance, and been infected with such greed, and been coveting other men's property without it being known? or is it rather, as the truth is, because I have given no handle for a lawful charge against me, nor caused annoyance to anyone soever? As to the devout p. 39.
Leontius, it was not out of need as you think that we raised him to the honour of the presbyters' seat, but because we wished to honour the man. And this is not the first time (I speak with God himself as witness), but long before this was in my mind, even before your love of God was raised to the high-priesthood. We had in fact made the acquaintance of the man and he was known to us by letters, even while we were practising the philosophic life in Palestine. However, I did not even know that the said

Leontius himself is among those that are in such high esteem with you. Neither had you ever bestowed upon him such laudatory expressions as you now do in your letter, nor had we ever learned that the stability of the holy church of the Apamenes was shaken by him. However, if the man is of such a character, and is among your friends and counsellors as you say, even one letter from your love of God is enough to win him over: and if he desires to live in the city of the Apamenes we will in no way prevent him, nor will we detain his devoutness, even though it was thought that we needed him for something. But that we should commit the unholy and uncanonical action of driving him out against his will,
p. 40. and turn the honour into a shame, neither you nor any other intelligent man like you will judge to be right. If you wished to raise the man to the priesthood as you say, the time past would have suited you equally well for this purpose. I consider that the grace of ordination receives no difference in similitude from the fishing-net, which is thrown into the sea of the world or into worldly matter by the Spirit itself: and that it is one, though divided among the nets of many fishers; among whom are Peter and James and John and Andrew, and all who fed the churches after them. All did not catch the same persons, but one caught one, and another another: but the grace of the fisher was one, because the faith also is one, and the church under the whole heaven of those who hold the same things is one. That therefore which

was done in the case of the devout Leontius is the action of the Holy Spirit, not of us. For it "bloweth where it listeth,"[1] as is said by our God and Saviour. If therefore you also catch one of the Antiochenes in your net, we shall find no fault at all with your fishing, but we shall praise the Holy Spirit which distributes to each man individually its own grace, and does everything in an ineffable manner and as it lists. Indeed in this frame of mind we pray that John also, the eloquent scholastic, the son of Matronian of illustrious memory, and the eloquent and Christ-loving p. 41.
scholastic Sergius may be enrolled in the order of those who minister to the Lord, and that they may adorn the church and be adorned by it and praise Christ. This I remember to have told your love of God also many times. And it was and is in my mind to raise the eloquent scholastics Peter and Maximin also to the priestly order; and I do not know through what reasons, known as they are to the wisdom that passes understanding, I have not yet been able to carry out what I intended. But for this also I am waiting for sanction from above, and divine inspiration. However I shall not dispute whether they are to be drawn in by my hand or yours: but so far am I from being jealous of you in respect of the fishing, that I will even help you and catch hold of the net with you above. Every matter whatever that is not contrary to the canons surely urges us to give help and to act

[1] John iii. 8.

in unison with one another. How is it anything but shameful that, while those who hunt birds reckon the air common property, and fishers, as I have said, the sea, we should dispute about things that lie not in our power but in God's? However, not to use many words and interfere with the moderate length of the letter (I think that even what has been written has gone beyond a moderate length), if the devout Leontius acquiesce in your wish as you say, we will consent, and will not retain him against his will: and this as
p. 42. a concession to you, and in order to show that, in things such as these, it is not our endeavour to subserve to the best of our power human purposes, but to walk according to the divine laws only.

513-8. 6. *Of the same to Nicias the bishop.* (*From those during episcopacy, from the 3rd book the 171st letter.*)

A wicked and unlawful action, one that conflicts with the laws of the catholic and apostolic church, has come to our ears. We hear that some of the inhabitants of the hamlet of Minidus and Uaris have presumed to sail westwards, and to receive an unhallowed ordination from those who hold the opinions of Nestorius and cut our one Lord and God Jesus Christ into a duality of natures after the ineffable union, an ordination which is invalid not in one way only but in many, and is reckoned as if it had never taken place: since, even if those who laid the presumptuous hand upon these men had

been orthodox, they ought not to have ordained in another parish or rather in one outside their boundary, in violation of discipline; and that while we by the grace p. 43.
of God are not charged with any heresy. This the holy canons plainly declare both in intention and in words. Therefore let your love of God make the purport of the sacred canons known to all in the neighbourhood of their parish, and proclaim them stripped of all the honour and rank of the priesthood and diaconate, and prohibit those who are in communion with us or rather with the right faith from associating with these men, that they may not communicate in the impiety, and call down upon themselves the wrath from God.

7. *Of the same to Castor, bishop of Perga. (From those during episcopacy, from the 3rd book the 232nd letter.)* 513-8.

The order of devout subdeacons in your see has asked a certain petition of us, which does not pass beyond the holy canons, but is contained within the fathers' landmarks as the sacred scripture says. For your sanctity well knows that there is a legal commandment in Moses, or rather a commandment of Christ who spoke through him, "Thou shalt not remove the landmarks that are from of old, which thy fathers set up."[1] What this is it is necessary for

[1] De. xix. 14.

us to say clearly. Those of the said order of sub-
p. 44. deacons who presented the petition to us say that they are greatly contemned and insulted by the readers and *psaltai* or singers of the holy church that is under you, inasmuch as they are trying to seize their place by violence, and seek to grasp for themselves the first rank, contrary to every consideration of justice and the law that prevails in the holy churches. Everywhere under the sun the order of subdeacons ranks before that of readers: both when named in the sacred tablets, and in the reception of the divine body and blood of Christ: and no one will anywhere see a reader mentioned before a subdeacon by the sacred voice of those that proclaim. Therefore your love of God also must preserve the same order, and not be so negligent as to place discipline second to the covetousness of individuals. You, who are a teacher and expounder of the divine words, are not unaware that even in the hosts that are in heaven there are certain ranks and degrees which are ranked before one another, those which are high as well as those which are low, those which ascend as well as those which descend. For Paul who was caught up to the third heaven shows this, when he writes to the Colossians and says, "Whether they be thrones or dominions, whether they be principalities or powers,"[1] and by such names shows that there is some order which bestows fair adornment[2] even upon the heavenly and invisible spirits, and thence descends to

[1] Col. i. 16.

[2] Misunderstanding of εὐκοσμία.

the church also, which was founded by God the Word p. 45.
who became incarnate and made the things that are seen and the things that are not seen, but differs in no way in its similitude from heaven, by reason of the great mystery of religion that is every day administered in it Wherefore also the same wise Paul in his epistle to the Ephesians writes thus about it: "And he himself gave: some apostles: and some prophets: and some preachers: and some pastors, and teachers:"[1] and in another place, "For God" (he says) "set first in his church apostles: next prophets: next teachers;"[2] and all that follow. By all these things we are taught to honour order, and to shun disorder and confusion: which principle we urge your sanctity also to observe in this present matter[3] also, which gave occasion for this letter.

8. *Of the same to Timostratus the duke.*[4] (*From those* 518-8.
during episcopacy, from the 3rd book the 256*th* 258*th letter.*)

To me it appears something to be prayed for and desirable to communicate with your greatness by letter: and to return the greeting that is owed to you
as if it were some necessary debt, and not make this p. 46.
the accidental result of causes about which I am even

[1] Eph. iv. 11. [2] 1 Co. xii. 28. [3] κεφάλαιον.
[4] *Cf.* Zach. Rh. ix. 1 (Eng. transl., p. 222 note 2).

ashamed to write. Though I was glad to see your magnificence's recent epistle, it was in sorrow that I ceased the reading of it. For I found the cause or subject[1] of the letter to be grievous when tested by the divine purpose, and difficult and impossible and "after the flesh"[2] to speak in the language of scripture, and one that is sensually judged.[3] Whereas the divine apostle, or rather Christ who speaks in him, limits and restricts the gift of ordination under a certain threat, and says, "Lay thine hand suddenly on no man, neither be partaker of other men's sins; keep thyself in purity,"[4] by many the thing is considered as one of the ordinary trades, that of a smith let us say or a carpenter, or as some office that brings with it the gift of sustenance, and an occasion of *dapane* or expense and a relief for need; as if it were not permissible for us to acquire the means of life from any other source than this. And the good men do not know that a man must pass through all the degrees of the church, and obtain some kind of previous training for priestly functions, and thus be admitted to ordination as presbyter or as deacon: and this because the thing is a matter of difficulty and rarely to be undertaken in accordance with the previously cited statute which says, "Lay a hand suddenly
p. 47. on no man, neither be partaker of other men's sins," and yet further enacts, "Keep thyself in purity"; and each of the additions declares the awfulness of the statute, and shows that the hand should in some way

[1] ὑπόθεσις. [2] 2 Co. i. 17 (?). [3] 1 Co. ii. 14. [4] 1 Ti. v. 22, 23.

be drawn to the head of those who are ordained under great necessity and unwillingly. In order to explain the first reason for which ordination is a formidable matter, these few words are enough for us. But I will add also a second reason, which is concerned with material considerations. This is that our holy church is very poor and needy, and that it is so much distressed and laden by the weight of interest, that it is hardly able even to hold up its head, but debts upon debts are added to its account, and interest upon interest is piled up against it. Of this all who live in the great city of Antiochus are witnesses: and I think there are not many even among those beyond its bounds who have not heard of the fact. And nevertheless certain persons in the royal city, and others in its neighbourhood, being worried by certain persons, do not cease every day so to speak writing to our meanness and asking for ordinations; and they think that this is not a matter to excite anger. And so foolish did this desire make some men, that they even made a show of desiring the dress of the priesthood p. 48.
only, and not seeking further to receive sustenance also: and, having once obtained their object, when the time of distribution came, they so to speak held out their hands before all the others: so that not only were those who made a mockery of divine things laughed at for the guile and treachery, but we also who were fraudulently deceived. These things I have been compelled to write to your magnificence, because I suffer in myself, and because I know that my

letter is addressed to a Christian, and to one who is capable of sympathizing with me and is perhaps also able to hold out a hand to me who am wearied and stupefied like a man who is being strangled by creditors, and am compelled to find sustenance for need without sufficient incomes and revenues, considering the immoderate extent of a demand that is pious indeed, but still difficult to satisfy on account of its frequency. *The end.*

513-8. 9. *Of the same to Stephen, bishop of Tripolis.* (*From those during episcopacy, from the 8th book the 276th, 277th letter.*)

Sinful and vile man though we are, nothing pleases us so much as to try to do everything that we wish to
p. 49. do with reason. Wherefore also we accept and praise your love of God for having been in doubt with regard to one of the paragraphs[1] that were written by us: regarding which we must by all means make a canonical answer; for it is written, "The lips of a priest shall keep knowledge, and they shall ask for law from his mouth."[2] What is the question which you ask because you were in doubt? Whether the devout presbyter Stephen ought to be reckoned among the holy clergy of the holy church in Tripolis, when he does not bring with him a dimissory letter from him who ordained him.

[1] κεφάλαιον.

[2] Mal ii. 7.

Now in the first place we hear that the man was ordained by force, and that he recoiled from or objected to an ordination outside the bounds, because he cannot live in a strange city which is not his own. And in the second place, even if this which we have stated is not the fact, we ought to know that those who do not hold to the orthodox faith, and therefore to the pure communion of our apostolic throne, have no share in strict canonical form, and we ought not to seek a dimissory letter from these, as if it were something necessary and required by law, or any other canonical requisite, when men flee from association with these, and come over to the sound teaching. This we may learn easily and without trouble from the epistle of the holy Cyril (every utterance of whom one would say is a law of the church) to Nestorius, in which he asserted himself to be in communion with all who had p. 50.
been separated by him, and had received from him either a ban of excommunication or a decree of deprivation, in these words: "But we are all in communion with all who have been separated by your devoutness and deprived on account of the faith, laymen and clergymen."[1] Do therefore the things which have been decided by us to be right without any doubt or hesitation, and know clearly that, if we had not taken much account of the saintly memory of Severus the presbyter whose is the lot of the saints, we should not perhaps have written to you any such thing. For your love of

[1] P.G. lxxvii. 108.

God must be assured that it is our earnest endeavour and desire not to write anything at all to the God-loving bishops under the apostolic throne about ordination, or about the enrolling of individuals in the order of the clergy, unless perhaps some just cause somewhere arise, as we see to be the case in the present instance also to which we are now referring. As to the venerable cross remaining fixed before the house of Theodore the illustrious governor and *vindex* after the former fashion, let your sanctity make it your earnest concern that it do so. It is the duty of bishops like you to cut short and to restrain any unregulated
p. 51. movements of the mob, if they should indeed occur, and to set themselves to maintain all good order in the cities, and to keep watch over the peaceful manners and customs of those who are fed by them. *The end.*

513-8. 10. *Of the same to Eucharius the bishop. (From those during episcopacy, from ——— book the* 142*nd,* 143*rd letter.)*

The transactions in the Christ-loving, believing city of the Paltians concerning Firminus have come to my notice, and I have agreed to them. Otherwise you would not have written, as may with most probability be inferred. It is however impossible to pass sentence upon a guilty man before he has had an opportunity of defence, having his accusers also face to face as is written.[1] Therefore, as form requires, our judgment

[1] Ac. xxv. 16.

is that the man who has sinned be sent here, and the actual men who are able to convict him, and to confirm the transactions regarding him, so that in this way we may cause him to be subjected to canonical sentences. For it is written, as your love of God who teach others p. 52.
also knows, "The innocent and righteous thou shalt not slay, and thou shalt not acquit the wicked."[1] *The end.*

11. *Of the same to the archimandrite of the monastery of Bassus. (From those during episcopacy, from the 3rd book the 345th letter.)* 514-8.

The letter of your love of God which has just been brought to me I have taken into my hands, and received as yours. For I rejoice and exult when I read your name even on the mere outside address, and I am brought to a more lively memory of your holy monastery, and draw away my thoughts from the worry of affairs, and in this way am refreshed and comforted. But, when the things written met my eye, I was astonished, and wondered how it could have come into your mind to make a profitless and impossible request. The devout Cosmas, who has just died, I instituted bishop of the city of the Apamenes, because I trusted to the report of others concerning him and their partiality on his behalf. For I confess to your holiness

[1] Ex. xxiii. 7.

that I never had any confidence in him. Accordingly during all the time previous to my coming to this city p. 53. of Antiochus it can in no case be shown that I addressed a letter to him; but it was the religious presbyter Theodore who used to write to him. But for what reason I would not consent to write to him it is not proper to the present time to say. However, as I said, I instituted him bishop, thus adding yet another to my sins. For what blasphemous utterances he vomited forth, and what darts he hurled against heaven God who heard knows. In plain language, not to make a long story, after many roundabout methods and entreaties on my part, and tears unsuited to the Holy Spirit, after alleging one reason and another, and at last bringing in his bodily infirmity also, he resigned the bishopric. Thenceforward the whole position was an insoluble difficulty to us, and full of doubt. For it was not only on account of the mistake made in his case and the words blasphemously put forward by him that there was cause for weeping, but also owing to the question in what way the affairs of the Apamenes would have to be administered: for in such a state of confusion all counsel was helpless. The God-loving bishops who in accordance with the statutes of the church were residing at that time in the city of the Antiochenes, being present, exhorted me to receive him as wishing to resign. And, since it was impossible for one church to be united to two men at the same time, he drew up petitions of resignation, saying of himself that he was no bishop and no clergy-

man, nor did he hold any other degree in the ministry. And, after this had taken place, the God-loving bishop Peter was thereupon instituted. How then is it possible to undo, as you ask, a thing that was carried out with so much caution and without anger? Assuredly, if the transaction which renders Cosmas not a bishop is not maintained, it results that the God-loving Peter was uncanonically instituted, and was given to a church that had already received a bishop. Accordingly it is plain that the resignation of the often-mentioned Cosmas tends to establish the ordination of the God-loving bishop Peter. But I for my part am wondering who advised your sanctity to ask this. Does anyone intend to clothe the dead man in that of which in accordance with the ordinances of the Holy Spirit that cannot be rejected he voluntarily stripped himself? or does anyone wish to mention him as a bishop? What therefore the wisdom of such a request is I am unable to understand. And what a time was it for a man's resignation to be recalled after his decease! Again, as to the fact that I went out to the devout Cosmas after he had fallen ill, I wish the sequence of events not to be unknown to your sanctity. Some of the zealous
brethren came up to me and begged me to go to him, p. 55.
on the ground that he himself was asking for this. But I said, "This cannot be. With a man who is not in communion with the holy church, I do not consider that I myself have any communion." And, though those who made the entreaty persevered, I would not consent: and I was so firm that for three whole days they urged

the point, and I did not yield. But at last one of those who were with us, the religious deacon father Elijah, began to say that perhaps he wished to repent, and to receive the oblation from my sinful hands. When this was said, I considered that I should bring myself under the judgment of God, if I did not on this consideration consent to the request itself: and in this hope I went to visit the afore-mentioned man. However, knowing as I did his unyielding character, I said to those who were with me: "Believe me when I say that I am going out against my will and without any confidence."[1] And, when I had gone, I made a prayer in the expectation that he would repent: but to give him a greeting or to ask a greeting from him I would not consent, far be it! For with what reason could I have given a greeting of peace to a man who refused the mystical peace before the holy altars and communion with us? Woe is me if I give a bodily greeting to any man when my soul does not agree to the greeting. When therefore we had sat down and
p. 56. none of the things that were expected was said by him, but, though he could not articulate, he kept urging and inviting us to enter upon a long conversation, while I for my part considered it a sin for us to enter upon a contentious and profitless conversation while the man was on the point of giving up the ghost, I rose, and prayed to God in private to forgive me the inconsiderate visit. To a man who was so disposed I

[1] πληροφορία.

ought not to have gone out at all. Even when he was dead and many thought I should go there, I did not go; considering that "everything that is not of faith is sin,"[1] according to the words of the Apostle. For I for my part consider a man who separated himself without reason from our orthodox communion an enemy not a brother, even if he is deceived by the devil, who "is transformed into an angel of light,"[2] by considerations that are rather upon the right side. For I hear the Lord say, "He that is not with me is against me: and he that gathereth not with me scattereth."[3] Indeed by the prayers of the saints and of your holiness, when church histories and the labours of the holy fathers from the coming of the great God and our Saviour Jesus Christ down to this time come before me, I find that this present condition[4] of the holy churches in the East and in Egypt is purer than the condition[5] p. 57.
in former times, when the facts are examined side by side. They therefore that trouble the simple "shall themselves bear the judgment whosoever"[6] they are, and shall themselves "give account in the day of judgment,"[7] when "he shall come who knoweth the hidden things of darkness and revealeth the counsels of the hearts."[8] As for me, may I have no part with such men, either in this world or in that which is to come! For, shunning as I do harshness of speech, I do not wish to declare in detail what is the judgment

[1] Ro. xiv. 23.
[2] 2 Cor. xi. 14.
[3] Mt. xii. 30.
[4] κατάστασις.
[5] καταστάσεις.
[6] Ga. v. 10.
[7] Mt. xii. 36.
[8] 1 Co. iv. 5.

of those who turn aside. Wherefore also I am urgent in entreating every one of those who have been involved in the error not to continue in the plausible strangulation of this righteousness, and hold aloof from the life-giving communion of the holy mysteries. And so forth. *The end.*

514-8. 12. *Of the same to Cosmas and Polyeuctus and Zeno the presbyters.* (*From those during episcopacy, from the 3rd book the* 354*th letter.*)

Even in the case of things that are acknowledged and manifest we are not justified either by the form of
p. 58. human laws or by the ordinances of the Holy Spirit in judging on the statement of one side. Wherefore neither did we consent to agree to the things that were written by your devoutness; not because we do not believe you, but to preserve the appearance that befits those who have been entrusted with the task of judging such matters. The right and proper course would have been for your love of God to come as far as here: and then we would have summoned the other side also to come to us, and the truth would have been determined. Or, if they remained away and did not come when summoned, then the provisions laid down in the laws regarding those who remain away would have been plain and would have followed upon the act. For our own desire is not to leave the matter unheeded and unsettled. If the saintly Isidore, bishop of

the city of the men of Chalcis, had been present, we would have yielded to him the duty of giving judgment concerning places and persons in his jurisdiction. But, as he is absent, it is therefore absolutely necessary that we should ourselves, as I have said, lay down a just conclusion of the questions that have been stirred. *The end.*

p. 59.

13. *Of the same to Entrechius, bishop of Anazarba. (From those during episcopacy, from the 3rd book the 397th, 398th letter.)* 513-8.

I do not know whether I should lay the blame of the events that are happening upon my sins, or upon the operation of an evil demon. Though there is nothing else that I have had so much at heart or for which I have prayed so much as that every Christian should conduct himself blamelessly, but especially those who are high-priests, giving no cause for reproach or blame against themselves, but being "in everything a pattern of good works, in gravity and in holiness," as the Apostle says, "in order that he that is of the contrary part may be ashamed, having no evil thing to say of us,"[1] I see that not once only but twice also I am worried about the same matters. Indeed, though some of the devout clergymen of the holy church of Flavias had presented to us certain accusations upon

[1] Tit. ii. 7, 8.

certain subjects[1] against their God-loving bishop, and we managed the affair ourselves, and brought things that else would have been troublesome to a peaceful
p. 60. *typos* or conclusion and so settled them, now again old men bowed down with age have risen up to make more serious charges, men who, if one may so say, struggle against life itself, and live in utter poverty and need : if one were to call them a pitiable sight, the expression would not be amiss. The statements made by them are many and various. Still for my part, again following the same practice, I wished to stop their accusation if it were possible : but, as they went on saying the same things, I proposed to commit the hearing of the case[2] to your holiness. But, since they objected, and said that their life would be no life for them, if the religious Procopius their bishop did not come here, I have adopted a middle course (I do not think that others either will think the coming to us an easy thing) and resolved to send the religious Theodosius a presbyter of our apostolic see that he may examine the facts in conjunction with your love of God, and a decision consonant to the canons may be given by you, and a conclusion reached upon each of the subjects[1] with the greatest possible accuracy. But at the same time we have resolved to say this much, that the said religious bishop Procopius should not, after the first warning, have received a gift at ordinations
p. 61. on the pretext of making a profit for the church, as he

[1] κεφάλαια.

[2] ὑπόθεσις.

used to say, and again been detected in the same practices, as those who make the accusation against him say: nor should he have named Lampetius[1] at the divine sacrifice, a man who was infected with the heresy of Adelphius, and for this reason was condemned at Commanus in Armenia, as the minutes[2] of the records[3] of that synod also show. Indeed, to pass over old matters, it is easy for your love of God to learn what canonical discussion the abominable flock of the Adelphians received in Second Cappadocia, seeing that the saintly Soteric bishop of the city of the men of Cæsarea and the holy bishops who sat with him, from Cappadocia and from Pontus and from Galatia, then put forth a decision worthy of the priesthood against it. Of this same heresy the outward token is greed and immodesty and a mad desire of vain glory, owing to which they pride themselves in attracting admiration and receiving in secret the evil spirit: and, what is most important, the fact that, infected as they are with extreme godlessness, and wearing as they do a deceitful mask of hypocrisy in all things, they put forward this deception also, that their heresy is not a heresy: for they count up all the p. 62.
heretics in order and anathematize them, but Adelphius they honour by silence. The celebrated freedom from passions of which they boast they do not display at all: and concerning matters on which charges are made against them they give no satisfaction,[4] but from

[1] *Cf.* vit. Sev. p. 28. l. 24. [2] πρᾶξις. [3] ὑπομνήματα. [4] πληροφορία.

matters on which they are not accused they gather the reputation of not being godless. It lies therefore with your love of God in conjunction with the religious Theodosius the presbyter of our apostolic see to see that the whole matter is as I have said carefully examined, and to make known the result of the examination to us also, in order that on all sides the appearance of the church may be preserved blameless. And another thing seems to me to be urgently demanded by piety, I mean that these unhappy men be not vexed by a long and useless session, who from necessity, as I believe, have made the accusation; and that they should not support themselves at their own expense, but that they should receive double the necessary daily sustenance from the holy church of which they are members. Another matter too you must set right without dispute before the trial itself, a thing which appeared to me absolutely incredible and still even now appears so: I mean that the said men themselves should be enrolled in the sacred number of the clergy, their names having been expunged, as they say, for this reason and no other, because they were able to have recourse to the apostolic throne on account of the things which they suffered and the wounds that have been
p. 63. inflicted on them. That this, if it is true, surpassing as it does all presumptuous audacity, needs canonical punishment, I leave to your love of God to reflect. *The end.*

14. *Of the same to Antoninus, bishop of Berrhœa.* 514-8.
(From those during episcopacy, from the 4th book the 65th letter.)

We were glad to see even the illustrious tribune Antiochus inasmuch as he came from you, and we encouraged him to converse constantly with us, and to ask for everything that is in our power, and is for the spiritual assistance of your love of God. And we praised him to the God-loving bishop Thomas, and, although we are sinful and vile, we repaid him by prayers. We have come to believe that the man who made the happy mistake in the address of the letters did not fall into the error without some divine providence. For this showed clearly that the two of us are wrapped up in one another, being joined together by the love that is in Christ, and that we have all things common according to the commandment,[1] and have nothing of our own. Know however that the letter which properly belonged to you but was addressed to us we have not yet received. As to the ordination at Chalcis (I call the truth to bear witness to my words) no letter has come to us, or any information or indica- p. 64.
tion. But, if you have in a philosophic manner been brought to a state of exasperation on account of the things that have happened among you, there is no cause for wonder : since this also is proper to the orderliness of your habits and to your discretion, which allots all

[1] Ac. iv. 32 (?).

things to the times suited for them. But, since we know that your holiness delights in words of admonition, and that you are eager to amass all things that conduce to the salvation of the soul and the acquisition of divine wisdom (for it is written, "The ear that heareth the reproof of life shall dwell among the wise,"[1] and, "He that keepeth reproof loveth his soul"[2]), we say with boldness the things that seem to us to be right. You also were not ignorant that those who managed Simeon whose soul is at rest (for he did not rule himself but was ruled by others) performed no sacred or ecclesiastical action except for money or under the influence of passion. For, if one may so speak, they were not known for virtue to any one of all the men who live in the East. To men such as these therefore you should never have lent your undefiled and sacred right hand, when they were making a division and presenting men for the sacred order of priests, especially when the ordination, performed as
p. 65. it was just before death, contained in itself a great fraud. For how was it possible that a man who in time of health never did anything sound in such matters should in time of disease be in any but a diseased condition for examining the question of propriety? For that he was awake when he gave you permission neither do I dispute: I consider your testimony more trustworthy than all oaths and every ground of confidence. Still, since you thirst to hear things that

[1] Pr. xv. 31 (Hex.). [2] *Id.* xvi. 3.

profit, there is a further point which I will not omit, that it would have been a thing in accord and very consonant with the devoutness of the rest of your life to tremble and hesitate to undertake ordinations that belong to others, and by actual deeds to show that it is with order and in all fear and only from actual necessity that you minister and serve even in those that belong to yourself. As to the question whether the ordination performed on the said persons ought to hold good or not, we believe that, after we have learned the whole character of the action and of the persons, we shall give a decision that agrees with the judgments of God, and shall urge that this hold good: not because we do not think the fruit of your blameless hand perfect (this is beyond doubt), but because we are examining the question whether those who received the grace are worthy or not. In any case we think your love of God will be contented, since you do not even desire to be contented with things other than those with which God is contented.
If our wretched discourses be copied out, we will send p. 66.
them to you. For we have ordered them to be copied out, though we have not in plain fact even a man to copy. Before this present letter was closed, the God-loving Isidore bishop of the men of Chalcis arrived in our city: and this has been added to the things written, because we honour the truth before all things. And now it will be our endeavour to learn from him also what his disposition is with regard to the same aforesaid ordination. *The end.*

513-8. 15. *Of the same to the same Antoninus, bishop of Berrhœa.* (*From those during episcopacy, from the 4th book the 72nd letter.*)

That the presumptuous deeds of the impious Jews are beyond all forgiveness, and such as to stir and excite any soul to just wrath, even one that is not easily roused, if only it has been initiated in the doctrines of piety, is plain and manifest. But that those who like you are lovers of God and at the same time intelligent persons ought to handle such things in a wise way you have already shown in your epistles,
p. 67. the epistles to us and to the glorious patrician and lieutenant of the general of the East excellent in all good qualities, your uncle.[1] Hence also we met together, and discussed the whole matter in conjunction, and endeavoured as far as possible to remove beforehand and prevent the evils that were about to spring up, and we set down what as the outcome of our deliberations appeared to us to be expedient and made this known to your sanctity. The indication given by their excellencies and by us who discussed the matter in common with them is therefore complete: but it will be a matter for your consideration to arrange the action to be taken on a proper footing. No punishment is severe enough for the arrogance of the Jews: but still men who stand at the head of the teaching of

[1] θεῖος. There is nothing in the words to show whether this refers to the lieutenant or to the general; but, as the *Mag. Mil.* was probably Hypatius (i. 40), the uncle of Antoninus would be the lieutenant. *Cf.* p. 125.

piety ought not to look at what they ought to suffer, but at what we ought to refrain from doing. This I say, not in order that we may take no account of the divine laws, but that, while singing with David, "I have hated them that hate thee, Lord, and against thine enemies have I been wroth,"[1] we may also have in our mind at the same time the commandment of Moses that says, "Fathers shall not die for children, neither shall children die for fathers: every man shall die in his own sin,"[2] and not[3] as is said by one of the wise men without, "The thing that so-and-so is so-and-so is not." *The end.*

16. *Of the same to the same Antoninus, bishop of Berrhœa. (From those during episcopacy, from the 4th book the* 101*st letter.)* p. 68. 513-8.

As for the accusation in the matter of the silence after the feast of salvation, which you attack as if it had been a violation of justice, I shall be acquitted by the experience of fact. For indeed before the charge itself was made at all I had already sent a letter to your sanctity by John the eloquent scholastic. Nevertheless you must know that the greeting which is given at the festival of the saving Resurrection should always begin by a letter from you, as is the established rule with regard to the other God-loving bishops also. How is it then that, when you had not yet cast the

[1] Ps. cxxxviii. 21. [2] De. xxiv. 16.

[3] This clause is perhaps corrupt: the negative seems superfluous.

seed, you were thinking about the things that spring from that? With a clever jest at our poverty or our need you said that the devout Mark came to us in order to give presents, not in order to receive anything, and therefore we thanked your sacred soul in this matter also, and readily showed towards him too all the duties of love without expense, making the intercourse with him to consist of a cheerful face, a serene
p. 69. aspect, and gentle speech, and repaying the presents brought by him with torches and spices. Also on the subject[1] of the estates that are near the hamlet called Beth Remsha but of right belong to your holy church, we are exerting all our ability, and will cause measures to be taken that will accord with justice and also satisfy you. As to the Jews, as soon as I received your letter and found a convenient time, I thought good to prescribe a course to you in a few words. You must apply the distinction made by the apostolic laws of the wise Paul, who in speaking of matters relating to us cries, "Avenge not yourselves, my beloved, but give place unto wrath," and "'Mine is vengeance and I will repay,' saith the Lord,"[2] but in speaking of presumptuous deeds against God says, "If a man despise Moses' law, he dieth without mercy at the mouth of two or three witnesses; of how much sorer punishment think ye that he will be worthy who hath trampled on the Son of God, and hath counted the blood of the covenant whereby he was sanctified a

[1] ὑπόθεσις

[2] Ro. xii. 19.

common thing, and hath done despite unto the Spirit of grace?"[1] All who took part in the sin should, in my opinion, be subjected to a penalty, in order that even in future time the action taken may be a lawful example to those who dare to do the same things. Knowing therefore that this is our mind on this matter, p. 70
carry out what ought to be done with the help of God, even though hereafter we appear to write something that goes farther in the way of concession or is more ambiguous, avoiding however the appearance of contradicting ourselves. This I say on account of certain men who show, as they think, philosophy and clemency in the case of presumptuous deeds done against Christ. But I bring my words back like some ship to the prelude[2] or beginning of the letter, and again pray on behalf of your love of God with a disposition that is at the same time fervent and humble, one that exacts from us the debts of love and stirs our coldness to spiritual affection. For who is there, even though he be a man of no feeling, who would not be put to shame by such modest words as are written by you? *The end.*

17. *Of the same to Misael the chamberlain.* (*From those during episcopacy, from the 4th book the 103rd letter.*) 513-8.

For my part, when I was raised to this bishopric, unworthily indeed, but still by the judgment or per-

[1] He. x. 28, 29.

[2] προοίμιον.

mission of God, I intended to manage my affairs in
p. 71. a spiritual manner, and I had regard to the commandments of the gospel and the apostolic statutes and commands. And in the matter of ordinations I thought of nothing but the awful text, the cause of great fear, that says, "Lay a hand suddenly on no man; neither be partaker of other men's sins; keep thyself in purity:"[1] and as to interest or the avaricious system of loans it was my desire not to know even the very name of them. For I listened to the singing prophet, who at one time says, "He giveth not his money upon interest,"[2] and at another time again cries, "Interest and guile have not departed from her streets,"[3] things which, if one may so say, are known even to those who are not versed in the sacred writings. But, when I had had experience of the distressful state of affairs, and had seen in what a pitiable and wretched condition the fortunes of our holy church were, and that a great load of debts and of interest was hanging over it and threatening to overwhelm it, I forgot the spiritual laws: and it now seems to me a great thing to find men to lend; and meanwhile I make use of the term 'interest' as if it were some lawful name. But, as to ordinations, I no longer stand in awe of the strictness of the divine laws, nor will I in future allege this in excuse to those who beg or seek to ask for these: but, when I see the poverty on all sides, and that every year we are obliged to have some kind of

[1] 1 Ti. v. 22, 23. [2] Ps. xiv. 5. [3] *Id.* liv. 12.

collection in order to distribute among the devout clergymen whom we have the money for their support, p. 72.
I am afraid of the *œconomi* or stewards on account of the scantiness of our resources, and I publish the need up and down : though I should have alleged the strictness of the spiritual commandments. For those who worry me about this are very many : and each of them looks at his own request only, and does not know how many there are who desire to obtain the same things. And, as soon as one of them has been disappointed of his request or desire, he immediately becomes an enemy: there is no middle position. And hence springs implacable war: so that I should now, if it were possible, revolt even against this vain life itself. For all these men do not allow us to choose the good, and to carry out with circumspection the things that we wish, and content those who like you often give such commands in a pious spirit. Hence I have been compelled to cause annoyance to the glorious sacellar Eleutherius also, who has often thought fit to write to me about a certain person, sometimes personally, sometimes through those who manage my *apokriseis*. For I see that these presumptuous dogs seek a thing of this kind as if it were some quarry : so that, if they found a means of beginning, they would bark at me : while they do not consider the need that encompasses us, nor do they wait for the help of God, who Himself p. 73.
alone is able to heal our church that is groaning under many wounds, and to change need into abundance. For it is He who says by the prophet, " Behold! it is

I who bring it healing and cure and I will cure it."[1] Seeing that you know these things, you who are able to share our distress and are in character a lover of God, I beg you to offer a defence on our behalf based upon the facts themselves to those who are concerning themselves about anything of this kind. Especially satisfy the aforesaid glorious sacellar the lord Eleutherius, and inform his excellency that what is being done is not due to haughtiness, but to necessity, and to distress. Out of shame I have never dared to communicate with him by letter on this subject: but through your mediation I have now made my defence to him. Nevertheless I will to the best of my power use any convenient opportunity, and will perform as far as possible what he has commanded. *The end.*

513-8. 18. *Of the same to Entrechius the bishop. (From those during episcopacy, from the 4th book the 123rd letter.)*

The devout clergymen of the holy church in the city of Rhosus and the other inhabitants of it[2] have
p. 74. presented a petition to us in which they beg that that man may be instituted their bishop by grace from above and the ministration of your sanctity, in whose favour they shall themselves according to the legal custom make a *psephisma*. These were the

[1] Jer. xl. 6.

[2] So B. Correct the text.

contents of their petition: but their vote applied to one man: and they received from us a notice that they were to include three men well-known for virtue in the vote, and so present the *psephisma* to you, and hold your judgment in this matter final. This is in other ways pleasing to God, and is also the proper course. In fact we argued with them and said that on no other terms but these would your piety, whose endeavour it is in everything to follow after blamelessness as it is written,[1] be ready to comply. Wherefore also we immediately determined to draw up this letter of reminder to you. *The end.*

19. *Of the same to Solon, bishop of Seleucia in Isauria. (From those during episcopacy, from the 4th book the 149th letter.)* **514–7.**

The constant evil things that are being done in close succession and in various ways in Isauria counsel us to silence. But still, when we turn over in our p. 75.
mind the judgments of God, we are again distressed, and cannot keep within us the cause of the distress, and we are brought round to the necessity of speaking. We have been in the same state as Jeremiah, who said, "I said, 'I will not name the name of the Lord nor speak in his name'"; and afterwards he was confounded and broke through the restraint that was

[1] 1 Ti. iii. 2, vi. 11 (?).

upon his mind, and he changed his mind and said, "And it became in my heart as fire burning and blazing and flaming in my bones, and I am dissolved on all sides and cannot endure."[1] What indeed am I to do? Last year I compelled the God-loving bishop Paul of Olba to return to the flock which it has fallen to his lot to feed; and now again I see him being disturbed in the same way by certain men who are not rightly disposed, and in old age and bodily weakness visiting now one country now another and wandering about: and, although the man acquiesces in our counsel, he carries out none of the things that we determined to be right. Now the things that we so determined are these, points which upon their coming a short time ago the party of the God-loving bishop Epiphanius and Symbatius also promised in common to observe with all their might and to their best endeavour, I mean that each should remove from the sacred tablets the names of
p. 76. those who signed the impious deeds of Chalcedon, but, as to the others, should remain silent and wait for a fitting season for progress to excellence. For there is no objection to ascent, as Gregory the Theologian also somewhere says.[2] But, as the old man, I mean the God-loving bishop Paul whom I mentioned before, is of a more than ordinarily simple disposition, I do not know how it is that you have been frightening him like a child with the signatures of documents, and

[1] Jer. xx. 9. [2] Or. xix. 7 (?).

have thus thrown him again into perturbation, when you should have treated each man according to his own condition and character, seeing that satisfactory professions have been made in common, and there is no doubt about them. So long therefore as the man remains of the same mind, receive him readily and honour him, on account of his venerable old age. Again as to the dispute that he had with the God-loving bishop Hilarian about a monastery,[1] when we heard of it, we should perhaps have given a proper solution and decision, had it not been that he flew to the royal city, as we have heard, separating himself from communion with you, on account of the presumptuous and illegal deed of Callistus. For he charges him with interpolating or forging or garbling the letter that was sent by him[2] (I do not know what expression p. 77.
to use on account of the many methods of committing the crime). For, on comparing the signature of the letter that was produced with the other signatures of the aforesaid God-loving bishop Hilarian that are preserved here in synodal documents, we found them to be as far removed and as different from one another as sheep differ in appearance from elephants. And, to say nothing of the strictness of the canons, it is manifest to everyone that the laws of the Romans also, which contain excellent enactments upon these matters, fix beheading as the punishment:[3] and this is an offence against public law. We wish therefore that

[1] *Cf.* p. 27. [2] *Cf.* p. 18. [3] C.J. IX. xxii. 22 (?).

the man who has acted so impiously in this affair should for the present abstain from all sacred ministration: and, as soon as he comes back, we will submit the matter to examination; since even in things that are thought to be acknowledged we like examination: and then we will pronounce for the facts of which the truth is established, placing before everything the just judgments of the balance-scales of God,
p. 78. and trembling lest by sparing others we make ourselves liable to these. For we are not ignorant what punishments Eli the priest received because, when his sons outraged the divine sacrifice, he only reproved them as a father and did not as an instructor and a ruler punish them according to the law. We have heard that the clergymen in the same monastery, while under inhibition from the God-loving bishop Paul, made light of his inhibition, and took part in the ministration with the God-loving bishop Hilarian. Therefore we have determined it to be right that they also hold aloof for the present from the sacred ministration, until he comes and a thorough investigation of the matter is held. *The end.*

514-8. 20. *A letter of summons in the name of a synod to the bishops under the metropolis of Apamea.* (*From those during episcopacy, from the 4th book the 187th letter.*)

Having been summoned by the grace of God and by the behest of our pious king, we assembled before

the evangelical throne of the great Christ-loving city of Antiochus for the purpose of carrying into act whatever seemed good to his[1] serenity's God-loving p. 79.
sovereignty: and one among those who assembled with us was Peter the saintly bishop of the illustrious metropolis of the Apamenes; and, being moved by an affectionate disposition,[2] we were induced to ask his love of God how it was that not one of you was with him, as was in fact the case with the other bishops of the resplendent metropolitan cities. But he said that he wondered whether it was in ignorance of what had happened that we were putting such a question. He was sighing, but still he related how you separated yourselves from the common communion of us all (for it was not from his),[3] and that he left no method of inviting you to concord untried. And, having included a few of the things that were done as he said in a petition, he presented it to the saintly patriarch of the God-loving bishops of the East, asking his beatitude to take canonical steps against the offences committed against him by you, or rather against the common union of the holy churches. For we were in fact all met together in accordance with fair adornment[4] and ecclesiastical order. And, when we had heard the petition, the serious character of the things that have been done called for a decision suited to the circumstances to be put forth: for the above-mentioned

[1] Syr. "their."

[2] διάθεσις.

[3] *Cf.* Evag. iii. 34.

[4] Misunderstanding of εὐκοσμία.

God-loving bishop of the metropolis of the Apamenes
p. 80. made certain of the charges themselves almost stand before every man's eyes without needing testimony from without. But we, considering that we are ministers of peace, and that, as we are one body, it is our duty to travel along every path that does not tend towards schism, but summons those who have fallen away to sin to repent, believed it to be right that we should summon you canonically, and should urge you to make a defence for the sins that have been committed, and should give time for repentance, and to say farewell to thoughts that lead to division, and with fitness to cry out to you also the words of the prophet which say, "Stand upon the ways and see and ask for the paths of the Lord that have been from everlasting, and see which is the good way and walk therein, and ye shall find holiness for your souls."[1] For a man to sin is human. But after he has once sinned not to listen to the admonition of friends, who summon him to them in a manner befitting priests, gives occasion for the apostolic distinction that says, "Behold therefore the mildness and severity of God, on them which fell severity, but on thee the mildness of God, if thou continue in mildness: and, if not then shalt thou also be cut off."[2] For it is in fact not obscure, especially to those to whose lot it has fallen to feed churches, that the authority of the holy canons cannot remain a dead letter in such things, seeing that

[1] Jer. vi. 16.

[2] Ro. xi. 22.

"the catholic and apostolic church requires blamelessness."[1] *The end.*

p. 81.

21. *Of the same to the Master of the Offices. (From those during episcopacy, from the 4th book the 189th letter.)* 514-8.

The illustrious Rufinus, the well-tried servant of your high eminence, when he brought to our meanness your revered and pious letter, which summoned us to the city of the men of Heraclea, was unable to receive our mean answer, because he was detained by a disease of the eyes; which answer was a short time ago brought to your glory by the resplendent Leontius, who is also one of your slaves. But, now that he is about to go up to the royal city, in payment of my debt I greet your highness. And I report and announce to you that the God-loving bishops residing in this city thought it a right thing to warn those who were bishops in Second Syria, of Epiphania I mean and of Arethusa and of Rhaphania, by a letter of summons, and summon them to them, in order that they might be detached from the disorderliness of those who are heads of the monasteries in those parts, and have unreasonably broken away from communion with us, and that they might either convince the others or be willing to yield to what is right. And some of those who rejoice in schisms and divisions, p. 82.

[1] Mansi ii. 672.

and have often conspired and plotted against my mean self also, and do not escape the knowledge of anyone, though they themselves desire to do so, persuaded them not only to pay no attention to their summonses, but even to compose an insulting and unlawful document against the holy synod of God-loving bishops, a document that contains blasphemous expressions against God and against the dress of the priesthood. These things the afore-mentioned saintly bishops discussed with the sacred and venerable book of the gospels laid before them, as well as the other sins committed by them at different times, and they found them to be madly excited (?) against the holy canons and church discipline and against our pious king, as the transactions in their case in fact show; and they laid them under sentence of deprivation: knowing clearly that, if such offences were to be left without reproof, the ordinances of the Spirit would be trampled upon, and any man who is a hearer would rise in opposition to those to whose lot it has fallen to be heads of churches: and, as in the case censured by the divine Paul, disorder would prevail, and the foot would say, "Because I am not the hand I am not of the body," and the ear, "Because I am not the eye I am not of the body,"[1] and each of the limbs would
p. 83. renounce its proper place. For there is a canon which says thus; "Bishops who are summoned to a synod should not treat the summons with contempt,

[1] 1 Co. xii. 15, 16.

but should go and teach or be taught for the purpose of reforming the church and the rest. But, if they treat it with contempt, such a man will be bringing an accusation against himself, unless perhaps he stay away on account of illness."[1] But these gentle persons under consideration not only set this statute at naught, but also insulted with unlawful expressions the God-loving bishops who are assembled in the great city of Antiochus which after God is yours. They thought fit to call them "no bishops at all," and in unmeasured arrogance they uttered yet other fatuous words which I shrink even from taking upon my tongue. It rests therefore with your excellency not by negligence to allow us to be trampled upon by such men, and be calumniated by men who are seeking their own interests, but to report the truth to the pious Christ-loving ears of our pious king, and extend to us sinners, who pray for your salvation, the just help that you extend to all who suffer wrong. *The end.*

p. 84.

22. *Of the same to the fathers.* (*From those during episcopacy, from the 4th book the 231st letter.*) 516-7.

Since all the holy fathers, if we may so say, have written us many various letters, we considered it necessary to write in a common epistle to you what we have to say concerning the common state,[2] and to stir you all up to one harmonious petition and earnest

[1] Mansi ii. 571.

[2] κατάστασις.

prayer. But the matters which ought to be conveyed in writing to your sanctities in particular are these. You did not do well or worthily of yourselves in not sending the devout deacon Stephen. The proof that he was confined to bed, by which you tried to prove his infirmity, we as a mean and sinful man will perhaps accept: but I have no means of saying whether Christ has also accepted it. For he is in fact even now still the same who ordered the man who was paralyzed and had for the greater part of his life been confined to bed to take up his bed and walk. However we will say with Paul, "All forsook me." And we will readily add, "May it not be laid to their charge."[1] But it is a matter for your prayers that the other thing also which he says may be granted us, "The Lord stood by me and strengthened me." For to say the words which follow these is too great a thing for me, I mean, "In order that by me the preaching might be completed and all the peoples might hear."[1] But, since we have in fact come to
p. 85. mention that matter, we will say a few words about it also; since, when writing a common epistle to all of you, we forgot it owing to the multitude of subjects of discussion. Musonius, the uninstructed and presumptuous man, who takes no account of the judgments of God, after disturbing and upsetting Isauria has gone as we have learned to Alexandria. For, being infected with two very serious diseases,

[1] 2 Ti. iv. 16, 17.

with avarice I mean and with pride, he wished to be a legislator for the men of the whole province.[1] And he despised like a carnal man the smallness of his city (for to spiritual men the privileges of the priesthood are matters that cannot be balanced, and are not weighed by the size of the cities, but judged by the dignity of the sacred office), and, making the God-loving Solon bishop of his metropolis, a man unversed in affairs and otherwise peacefully disposed, his ally, he caused constant disturbances, requiring from each of the bishops *homologiai* or professions in writing concerning principles approved by him. He even went so far as to draw up a minute[2] in which it is stated that all the names of those who ministered in any capacity whatever, presbyters and deacons and monks and laymen, ought to be expunged from the sacred tablets: so that everyone thereupon shrank from this burdensome and endless statute, and thenceforward they talked to one another and said, "We are p. 86.
progressing by degrees; we shall also be required to be re-baptized and re-ordained as it is said." And all in the province,[1] being goaded by this idea as by some sting, rose against their bishops, and they upset things that had been rightly done before: insomuch as to name all who had been left out, and associate in communion with those who hold the opposite opinions: and, to put it plainly, to go over to the opposite party, and drive the bishops out of their own churches.

1 ἐπαρχία. 2 πρᾶξις.

While these things were going on, the gallant Musonius was sitting inside his house; for, though he is bishop of another city, he registers his fathers' house at Olba; and he resides for the most part either there or in the metropolis of the men of Seleucia; and he only creates disturbances and in tyrannical fashion lays down heavy and unendurable laws. This man we have now already for three years borne with all meekness, though we often whispered of his madness, and many times we reconciled him when he was lightly breaking away and turning backwards. Wherefore also, when the bishops were assembled here, the same Musonius accused some of them of behaving in
p. 87. an undiscriminating or unlawful manner. And, when these also turned round upon him and accused him in their turn of lending his money on interest contrary to the canons, he was convicted, and was silenced. And, whereas he ought to have repented of this, with great shamelessness he proclaimed the sin a virtue, saying that his church possessed nothing, and lamenting about poverty and need: in consequence of which we ourselves assigned to him from here a sum of twelve darics a year.[1] Having received this he went away, after communicating with us and making a promise to the bishop of his metropolis to go up also to the cities of Isauria that had gone astray, and to undertake labour for a good end. And, when he reached the province,[2] he again lay hid (?) in his usual

[1] *Cf.* p. 25.

[2] ἐπαρχία.

haunts, and did not stir his foot anywhere, and never once opened his presumptuous mouth that has no door as the proverb says,[1] and is learned only in arousing uncanonical contentions. Thinking this an occasion that provided him with a means of amassing base gains, he composed a letter to the devout presbyter Longinus who is with us, fishing for yet another sum of gold, and a contribution of sacred property. And, failing in this, he turned to men in Alexandria who are infected with an uncanonical disease like his and a madness of no ordinary kind: who themselves received him as a priest, like Micah whose story is p. 88
recorded in the Tribes,[2] him I mean of the hill-country of Ephraim: who, having made a molten image out of his mother's silver and set this up as a god, found a young man, a Levite, and, filling his hand, took this man as a priest, saying to him, "Abide with me and be unto me a father and a priest, and I will give thee ten pieces of silver by the day, and a pair of garments, and the necessaries of thy life."[3] Whence also we believe that both Musonius and those who shall receive him or have received him will suffer the same end as those who oppose the judgments of the Holy Spirit and pervert the right ways of the Lord. But, to establish what has been said, we have thought good to quote also out of his fatuity some words taken

[1] Pr. xxvi. 28.

[2] The Syriac name for Judges, from a confusion of *shafte* and *shabte*.

[3] Judg. xvii. 10.

from his actual letter that he wrote to the religious presbyter Longinus, words which prove the passions that lurk in him. They are as follows:[1] "But you remember that I said to you, 'The patriarch ought to have sent something to our church as treasures.[2] By this means the men themselves also become more enthusiastic. In this way Flavian also acted to the bishop of Germanicupolis, when he gave both robes and treasures[2] to the unholy Bisula, and he drew the inhabitants of his country to him.'" And again: "For, although we do not ourselves know it, we ought to take an example from the adversaries, how
p. 89. they show all energy and watchfulness in making presents to those who are in opposition to them and endeavouring to bring them over to them by a gift. For you are not unaware that nothing persuades unlearned persons[3] so effectually as a present and a gift." You see how, involved as he is in the passion of avarice, he puts forward the specious name of the church and the simpleness of unlearned persons,[3] decorating the passion with mild words as with colours. I have also many other letters of his that he wrote to me, from which it is clearly apparent how I sought to change his haughtiness by mildness, and after many toils and labours did no good. And at last, becoming weary, I handed him over to the judgments of God, because he wrought such disturbance, and gave to those who were standing in the right way turbid upheaval to drink. *The end.*

[1] *Cf.* p. 26. [2] κειμήλια. [3] ἰδιῶται.

23. *Of the same to Solon, bishop of Seleucia in Isauria.* 516-7.
(From those during episcopacy, from the 4th book the 270th letter.)

Your sanctity has acted rightly and has shown a disposition consonant to the divine canons in thinking it right to ask me about Musonius and Paul. But, p. 90.
seeing that they have left their own flock, and played the part of hirelings and not of shepherds, whatever else can one say except that it is necessary that these men should be stripped of all priestly authority, and that they should be cut off from the number of the shepherds? We know that our Saviour also says these words in the Gospel: "He that is an hireling and is not the shepherd, whose own the sheep are not, when he hath seen the wolf coming, leaveth the sheep and fleeth. And the wolf catcheth the sheep, and scattereth them. But the hireling fleeth because he is an hireling, and careth not for the sheep."[1] You therefore, in order that you may not be found liable to the very same punishments, are bound quickly to appoint shepherds for the rational sheep: for those that are at Meloe immediately and without delay, since, as I said, Musonius took to flight like a hireling, and made this excuse for his absence as you write (and we have heard others also who know state the same), though the canons do not allow a man to absent him-

[1] John x. 12, 13.

self from his flock on his own authority and without the consent of patriarchs or metropolitans: but for those at Olba after the winter season has passed, since it was for another reason that Paul set out for the
p. 91. royal city, and it has not yet been made manifest to what city or country he went when he returned thence. But it is known to everyone that, when the deprivation of men who have utterly neglected their own cities is lawfully effected and in accordance with the precepts of the holy canons, others are appointed in the places of those who have been deprived. But, if you resolve to ask our pious king about this, I mean whether the God-loving bishops in Isauria ought to assemble and discuss the matter, and to compose a clear epistle and to report to his hearing that the men who have departed have fled to those who are eager to support their schism,[1] you will be doing very rightly, and, as far as one can guess, not contrary to the intention of his[2] God-loving sovereignty. In my judgment this is a necessary and very advantageous step, and one which may show his[2] piety that we avoid the rocks on all sides, and keep to the royal road and to the unity of the holy churches. While writing these things we weep and groan, and do not rejoice at our brothers' fall, and we consider how, while Musonius was extending his eyebrows upwards and puffing out his cheeks, and devoting his attention only to judging others, we were
p. 92. unaware of the fact that he was feeding his belly, and

[1] *Cf.* p. 79. [2] Syr. 'their.'

that he was inflamed with the passion of avarice. We have also letters of his which lay bare his passions that are so shameful.[1] As to the question I have thought it best to refer to the magnificent Œcumenius, since I have great confidence in your perfection, and because you love the man just as we do. Moreover by referring the matter to a man who has already discussed this with us we shall escape the necessity of using many words; for we have no leisure, and we are not even able to take recreation owing to the multitude of subjects of concern. *The end.*

24. *Of the same to Theotecnus the* archiatros *or chief physician.* (*From those during episcopacy, from the 4th book the 293rd letter.*) 514-8.

The things that have been indicated or announced to us from the royal city are many and various. But the sum of them is this. The bishops who assembled there have separated without coming to an agreement, since the majority of them or, if one may so say, all except the Romans, were found to be orthodox, but were obliged to associate themselves with the state of affairs[2] prevailing in the royal city, the saintly bishops Eleusinius and Proclus having for the time run away. Some said that the object of their endeavours was not to accept the impious synod that assembled at

p. 93.

[1] *Cf.* pp. 25, 80.

[2] κατάστασις.

Chalcedon in respect of the definition of faith but "in respect of the rejection of Eutyches and of his doctrines."[1] But that this endeavour or trick is the action of heretics your Christ-loving eloquence also is not unaware. But there is yet another thing which it is right that you should know: that is that our pious king and the glorious Master of the Offices wrote to my meanness by Leontius the illustrious magistrian[2] who is called Tapitoleon to ask that the deprivation of those no-bishops and wicked men in Second Syria might be annulled. And I wrote in answer to this, "Since this is your pleasure, if they lawfully repent, the intention of the canons receives them, provided all the bishops who deposed them assemble together and canonically receive them." It is enough to say
p. 94. this much as in a letter and in a few words. For I forbear to say that a certain defence of the definition of the men who assembled at Chalcedon was also contained in the pious letter: against which again we further argued without any harsh speech, advancing the words of truth in opposition to the plausible pretexts there put together. Regarding the name of Nestorius, which has been included among the commemorations of the martyrs in the metropolis of the Tarsians, and has rightly scandalized you, we have written to the God-loving bishop Dionysius such things as are fitting and proper, and our words have no doubt come to the knowledge of your God-loving

[1] *Cf.* p. 5.

[2] *Cf.* p. 73.

intelligence. The present of a shoe woven of wool I have received, and as a sinner I have prayed that a reward for it may be given you from above, you who do well in mingling spiritual healing with material. For the gift is material: but the fact of the affectionate thought is spiritual, and therefore a thing that contains in it comfort for soul and body. *The end.*

p. 95.

25. *Of the same to Dionysius, bishop of Tarsus.* **513-8.**
(*From those during episcopacy, from the 4th book the* 331*st letter.*)

It has come to our ears that a presbyter in the village called Pessinus (?) has contracted a human affliction; and that, being harassed by the possession of a demon, he is wandering about and being driven to and fro through the land. And we have thought it right to warn your holiness to behave in a sympathetic and fatherly manner towards the man, but not to go on to allow the bloodless sacrifice also to be performed by his hands, seeing that the canons do not even allow communion in the divine mysteries to those that are possessed,[1] still less do they allow such to have any communion in priestly functions. For it may be that through this those who approach to receive also will hereby find occasion for some stumbling, and will approach the

[1] Mansi i. 45.

divine mysteries with doubt and hesitating thoughts. But we must be "without offence" towards every man in accordance with the apostolic statute.[1] *The end.*

p. 96.

515-7. 26. *Of the same to Solon, bishop of Seleucia in Isauria.* (*From those during episcopacy, from the 4th book the 338th letter.*)

Paul the bishop of Olba, as may be inferred from his so long and protracted absence, has done the work of a hireling and not of a shepherd, one who, when he sees the wolf coming, as the sacred book of the gospels says, "leaveth the sheep and fleeth: and the wolf catcheth and scattereth them; and he careth not for the sheep because he is an hireling and not the shepherd."[2] Henceforth therefore we also ought no longer to wait for a man of such unstable character as his (it is right for us to speak in this gentle language), but to settle the things that lie before us on a good basis, and in accordance with the purpose of the laws of the Spirit. The same Paul charged the God-loving Hilarian bishop of Diocæsarea with having performed an ordination, contrary to the holy canons, in a monastery which is not in his jurisdiction; and we thought it right to prohibit those who were ordained from exercising the sacred ministry until the details of the case[3] should be examined;[4] for the matter was not
p. 97. clear but in fact much involved and in need of ex-

[1] 1 Co. x. 32. [2] John x. 12, 13. [3] ὑπόθεσις. [4] *Cf.* p. 70.

amination and a correct decision. But now we have determined it to be right to release the said men from the inhibition and to allow them to exercise the ministry, since it is not possible to wait any longer for a man who has been absent so unreasonably and in a manner unknown to the church ordinances. Therefore your sanctity also, in accordance with the conclusion at which we have arrived, must now allow the men to perform priestly functions, reserving the examination into the doubt as to the monastery, and as to the ordination itself and those to whom the jurisdiction over this belongs for a future season, if the time should invite us to this. *The end.*

27. *Of the same to Musonius and Alexander* vindices 513-6.
of Anazarba. (*From those during episcopacy, from the 5th book the 74th letter.*)

It would have been best if you had both come to us and also gladdened our eyes by the bodily sight of you, and by this sight comforted me more. But, since you have public[1] business on your hands, and are thereby prevented from so doing, I support the sorrow thus caused by feeding on the spiritual sight only, and so lighten the loss. Wherefore also, as a token of p. 98.
undivided affection towards you, I have composed this one letter to both of you: in which I make known to

[1] δημοσίων.

you that the whole synod of the God-loving bishops of the East is united in the right doctrines and anathematizes all the heresies : among which are included those who divide our one Lord and God Jesus Christ after the union into a duality of natures, and the vain concourse of those who assembled at Chalcedon, the stronghold of this evil heresy, and the impious Tome of Leo (if one called him a cleaver of peace, the expression would be a fitting one). These things having thus passed in order (to speak with the permission of God), we have now drawn up a synodal letter addressed to the God-loving archbishop of the city of the Alexandrines John, inviting him to unanimity and pure communion. And we will write epistles in the same way to the others also, keeping everywhere to the royal road, and not turning aside to the right or to the left,[1] guided as we are by the great love of Him who is the guide and leader along this road. Concerning the faith and communion with the others, as far as it was possible to give information in a letter,
99. let this much suffice. If we ever meet together, you will know everything in greater detail and with greater clearness from actual experience. As to Martyrius the poet, whom you made the occasion[2] of the letter, I wish you to know that he is a trouble to me, and a nuisance. Indeed in the case of the others also who follow the same profession, and were enrolled in the holy clergy of the church that is with us, I have

[1] Nu. xx. 17. [2] Marg. 'skin'; B, 'whom you sent with the letter.'

debarred them from practising such poetry: and I am taking much trouble to sever this theatrical pursuit from ecclesiastical gravity and modesty, a pursuit that is the mother of laxity, and is also capable of causing youthful souls to relax and casting them into the mire of fornication, and carrying them away to bestial passions. But because of his repentance I rejoice with him, and because of the fact that he is a lover of the orthodox faith: especially since you who are careful scrutinizers bear witness in his favour. Let him therefore stay where he is, and not desire to return to this city. It is not possible for him to do so in my judgment: not from anger against him (far be it!), but because of the evil pursuit and the desire of avoiding the aforesaid injury. *The end.*

p. 100.

28. *Of the same to Philoxenus, bishop of Doliche.* 513-8.
(From those during episcopacy, from the 5th book the 66th letter.)

After your love of God had departed hence, and had left this great Christ-loving city, in the venerated days of the holy fast, many of the prominent men came up to my meanness, and presented to me a petition and a unanimous entreaty on behalf of the devout Romulus, asking that he might be allowed to conduct prayers without fear of punishment so long as he resides here. These were the actual words that they said, wishing to dispose me more to the side of mercy. But I said,

"On no account will I permit this, until his bishop" (meaning your love of God) "shall free him from his inhibition. For we must in all things observe the rules and ordinances of the church." I beg you therefore to do me this favour, and pronounce to me by letter the words of forgiveness, in order that I also may thus lawfully give him permission, and may fulfil the will of those who asked; who are every day, if I may so say, worrying me, and entreating me to assent to this easy and humane request. The position in which we stand I have described in writing to the saintly metropolitan the lord Philoxenus; and he will

p. 101. no doubt inform you of it, and will stir you up to offer prayers concerning the general state of things.[1] *The end.*

518-8. 29. *Of the same to the devout monks of the blessed lord Isaac.* (*From those during episcopacy, from the 5th book the 97th letter.*)

The trial concerning the affair of the magnificent Antipater has by your prayers passed away: and in accordance with the mercy granted us from above we have been delivered from this: the magistrates having given this one order only, that the said Antipater shall not be permitted to remove anything from the room in which he put his baggage, since you are ready to give satisfaction[2] on this point also. But now I am writing

[1] κατάστασις. [2] πληροφορία.

to your love of God about a matter which is for the common benefit, and tends to the advancement of the right faith and the preservation and extension of the holy churches of God in the East. The men of the camp[1] of Anasartha[2] by their *psephismata* proposed various persons in order that a bishop might be ordained for them; and I for my part determined that we would ordain the religious father Stephen, who is adorned with character and with faith, and, if one may so say, with all excellencies of virtues, bishop for the p. 102.
aforesaid camp[1]: not because we wish to honour the man, for I know that he shrinks from this, having more regard for his own profit; but, just as I paid no attention to this but complied with the judgments of God, in the same way I beg your holinesses also and him not to resist the grace of the Spirit which calls him. For the whole force of Christianity tends to this, that we should not have regard and respect to our own interests but to those of others. Moreover, it is also utterly unreasonable that, while we are displaying such contests on behalf of the orthodox faith, we should entrust the presidency of the holy churches to reprobate persons, men too who (which I pray may not happen), when tribulation or persecution has come, as the holy Gospel says,[3] are converted to impiety. Do your diligence therefore to obey this letter, and to send him whether he wishes or not: and be assuredly convinced of this,

[1] κάστρα. [2] *Cf.* Mansi vi. 1090; Wright, C.B.M. 756b.
[3] Mt. xiii. 21.

that, if another man, who is reprobate, be instituted owing to his delay, you will be responsible for the loss. Do not pass him over and wish to send me someone else from your holy cloister in his stead: for I will not consent even to look at anyone else. I have chosen the religious father Stephen as being one of those men-
p. 103. tioned in the *psephisma* by those who came from the aforesaid camp[1]: and for us to introduce someone else not included in the *psephisma* is impossible. I add also that neither have I myself confidence[2] in anyone else. This much we have written out of love. But, although we are a sinner, we have received, as you also with one accord confess, authority from Christ, who is God over all, to bind and loose: wherefore I wish you to know that, if you do not obey the words written above, you will be placed under a ban of excommunication; especially the devout Stephen himself, if he dare to resist this proposal. My reason for adding this after the completion of the letter is to show that it is from necessity that I come to adopt a decisive course of action. *The end.*

513-7. 30. *Of the same to the clergy of the metropolis of Apamea.* (*From those during episcopacy, from the 5th book the 135th letter.*)

Your love of God, marked out as you are by the orders of the holy clergy of the church, and addressing a

[1] κάστρα.

[2] πληροφορία.

bishop, and upon a spiritual subject,[1] ought not to have p. 104.
cited the rhetor of Greece in the preludes[2] or beginnings of your admirable letter. In due time Elijah the Tishbite, urged by the same zeal, will now say to you also, "Is it because there is not a prophet in Israel that ye go to inquire of the fly-Baal, the abomination of the gods of Ekron?"[3] Fitly also will the book of Proverbs reprove you which says, "Drink waters out of thy vessels and out of the spring of thy wells."[4] You did not make search in order to draw from the divine scripture a saying that would prove the swiftness and weakness of human life. For the prophet David says, "Our days pass away like a shadow."[5] And the divine Job, while playing the philosopher during the grievous trial caused by his suffering, said, "For we are of yesterday, and we know not":[6] and again, "My life was swifter than a runner."[7] We are not unaware that the wise Paul also often quoted the words of poets in speaking to certain persons. But the character of the hearers, who had not been instructed out of the God-inspired words, in itself made the use of testimony from these seemly in his case. The divine scripture should therefore have been enough for you, and you should not have started by making the beginning spurious and false. We therefore (for we must now return
to that which is more useful and more urgent) have p. 105.
been grieved at the decease of Isaac of religious

[1] ὑπόθεσις. [2] προοίμια. [3] 4 R. i. 3. [4] Pr. v. 15.
[5] Ps. cxliii. 4. [6] Job viii. 9. [7] *Id.* ix. 25.

memory, your bishop; and we have been distressed because he left the present life before he had maintained a contest on behalf of the doctrines of orthodoxy, which he proclaimed in writing and otherwise in this great Christ-loving city. However we submit to God, the orderer of such deep judgments. But the duty that remains for us is this; not to be negligent and leave your holy church without a shepherd during the days that are so venerated of the saving Passion and of the Resurrection of Christ. Make haste therefore and draw up quickly a *psephisma* in favour of three men of favourable repute and well known for virtue and, as it is written, "powerful men and religious, men that are just and hate pride."[1] But the powerful man is defined by the divine law as the man who through his life and conduct has power over the passions of the flesh, and possesses accurate and well-tried faith, which is greater than everything and is the foundation of our salvation. For the man who is to stand at the head of rational souls must have power in him, and is "able to comfort by sound teaching and to refute the gainsayers,"[2] as the Apostle, who had Christ speaking in him, handed down to us. This besides pleasing God will also gladden our pious king, seeing that he is
p. 106. much concerned for the apostolic faith, and has been brought up in such doctrines from his boyhood: who also in some sort did not praise our meanness for having delayed until to-day to institute shepherds for the cities

[1] Ex. xviii. 21. [2] Tit. i. 9.

that are in need, who shall feed them with understanding. Do not therefore look to worldly authorities, or under the influence of fleshly considerations put forth your vote in favour of certain men who live in a worldly atmosphere and need much purification, and ought not to be entrusted with the purification of the people and to offer the bloodless and rational sacrifice on behalf of the faults of whole congregations and as an expiation : for I hear that certain men among you dare to do such things, thinking to make a mockery of things that are divine and not subjects for mockery. Let no one think that I shall acquiesce in a vote in favour of such men, no not if I be very mad. It does not suit me because of the inconsiderate action of certain persons to "partake in other men's sins," as it is written,[1] or for no purpose to be sent to the eternal fire. When therefore you have duly drawn up a *psephisma* in accordance with our counsels, or rather according as the sacred ordinances and laws provide, let there come according to custom devout men, men modest in their conduct and earnest in character, such as are fitted to approach the apostolic throne and receive its judgment.

We learn that, while Isaac of saintly memory was breathing his last, certain persons, wishing to hide their own faults, by an evil action dared to remove from his office the man who was entrusted with the p. 107.
stewardship of the church property, and to put forward

[1] 1 Ti. v. 22.

others in his place, having unlawfully and contrary to custom taken the keys from him. Accordingly we have determined that the man who administered the stewardship before shall hold the same charge, and those who have now been introduced shall be turned out and remain somewhere at a distance, and that they shall not participate at all, lest by depriving him for a short time of his stewardship we seem to be giving him also some just reason for not giving an account for the whole of his administration in time past. *The end.*

515-8. 31. *Of the same a* hypomnestikon *to the bishops of Phœnice.* (*From those during episcopacy, from the 5th book the 236th, 237th letter.*)

How great account I take of the judgments of God I cannot explain in words. But, to speak after the manner of Paul, I call God to witness[1] that I pass the nights without sleep, and never cease being worn away by the cares of the days. And I tremble lest I administer the business of the apostolic see negligently, and have to bear the punishments that my negligence
p. 108. deserves, and be sent to the torments that are for ever and do not pass away. When I consider the divine words, spoken beforehand through the prophets, I am frightened and quake, and I think I hear God saying, "Therefore, shepherds, hear the word of the Lord;

[1] Ro. i. 9; 1 Th. ii. 5, 10.

thus saith the Lord of lords; 'Behold! I am against the shepherds and will require my sheep at their hands, and I will cause them to cease from feeding my sheep: and the shepherds shall not feed them any more, and I will deliver my sheep from their mouth and they shall not again serve them for food.'"[1] Thinking upon these words and such as these, and hearing God saying over and over again 'my sheep,' I mingle many tears with my thoughts, when I remember the religious Epiphanius,[2] who stealthily established himself in the Christ-loving metropolis of the Tyrians and stirred up many commotions there, when he should have betaken himself to this apostolic see and chosen things pleasing in the eyes of peace and done them, and so come back to the said city in brotherly and fatherly concord and agreement. Since therefore this duty has been neglected by him, and, desiring still even now to correct what has been wrongfully done, we have summoned him to us, we wish you to know that he is not allowed to perform any ordination until he has come to us and done everything required by law, and so yourselves to make p. 109.
a *psephisma*, as prescribed in the divine canons; and then after that one of those who have been duly selected will be chosen, who is able to rule the bishopric blamelessly and in accordance with the judgment of God. This also I was desirous of bringing to the knowledge of your holinesses, and I charged the religious Thomas and Basil deacons of the apostolic see to have in their

[1] Eze. xxxiv. 7, 10.

[2] *Cf.* vit. Sev. p. 30, l. 31; Evag. iii. 33; Mansi viii. 1074 ff.

hands this order in writing, and read it to each of you; that you are not to make a *psephisma* in company with the said religious Epiphanius for the nomination of any bishop, unless all things have first been carried out "with decency and with order," as Paul commands us[1] who consecrated the Gospel among the nations as he wrote.[2] We have concluded it to be a superfluous task to address each of the God-loving bishops, seeing that the urgency of the matter will not brook delay. Let no one among you therefore dare to transgress against this our warning in writing in any way whatever, knowing that he will incur an accusation of presumption and arrogance, and will be laid under bans of excommunication. This is in fact the reason why we resolved to send the God-loving Thomas and
p. 110. Basil deacons of the apostolic see, because it is our intention and prayer that all things may be carried out and performed in order. *The end.*

513-8. 32. *Of the same to John, bishop of Alexandria the less.* (*From those during episcopacy, from the 6th book the 154th letter.*)

The devout subdeacons of your church have made a complaint to the apostolic see, alleging that an old custom prevails in the holy church of the Alexandrines, which allows their order freedom from the obligation

[1] 1 Co. xiv. 40. [2] Ga. ii. 2.

of serving what are called 'weeks'[1] in your venerated bishop's house.[2] And we considered the statement in no way surprising if it is absolutely true, since in other holy churches also an exactly similar provision exists upon this point. Such matters are generally regulated in accordance with the customs of the holy churches, and the same model does not prevail in all of them. Seeing then that they both allege the custom in defence, and procure the things required to satisfy their necessities by worldly occupations owing to not receiving sustenance, your love of God should acquiesce p. 111.
in all these things, and not disturb that which is the custom by any innovation, unless perhaps some relief be given them as a counterpoise to the loss[3] that falls upon them. That a man ought not to serve at his own charges Paul also who had Christ speaking in him enacted: and to this he further added a saying that resembles it, I mean that a man who devotes himself to the altar should be supported by the altar;[4] and hence he gives the same decision in parallel cases also, and teaches that a man who is engaged in any work should also receive the means of life out of the very same business in which he is engaged. Therefore let the injunction also that has been laid upon them be removed, and the cells of their poverty opened, and the harsh acts that have been done obliterated by means of mildness in all things. *The end.*

[1] *Cf.* Mich. Cerul. Ep. 5, 5 ("ἑβδομαρίων πάντων ὑποδιακόνων"), and Ducange, *s.v.* ἑβδομαδάριος.

[2] ἐπισκοπεῖον.

[3] ζημία.

[4] 1 Co. ix. 7, 13.

518-8. 33. *Of the same to Dionysius, bishop of Tarsus.* (*From those during episcopacy, from the* 6*th book the* 186*th letter.*)

Time has, it seems, brought a new thing, I mean a
p. 112. military force demanding as if it were part of its pay that ordination be conferred by high-priests upon certain persons; for such is the unreasonable treatment which the God-loving bishop of Pompeiupolis has informed the apostolic see that he has received; and he says that soldiers with their swords held above his head almost threatened to take his head off, unless he laid his hand on the head of such-and-such a man. This illegal act therefore must by all means be annulled, and be considered as if it had never been done. For it is known to everyone that, where there is fear and a threat of death, and anything akin to these, and any of the passions that are created by the devil, there the descent of the Holy Spirit is assuredly prevented. I forbear to mention that as a result of this a very bad precedent will also be laid upon the churches, and we shall be required henceforth to perform solemn functions after the manner of tyrants, unless what has been wrongfully done remains void, as is in fact demanded by law. *The end.*

p. 113.

34. *Of the same a letter of summons to the bishops under Apamea.* (*From those during episcopacy, from the 7th book the 127th letter.*) 514-8.

Though we are weak and in deeds fail to keep to the way of the fathers, in that we are inclined to sloth and negligence, yet still as regards the orthodox faith, in accordance with the apostolic command, we prove ourselves to see if we are in the faith, and examine ourselves to see if Christ is in us:[1] and we know that in this we are not reprobate through grace from above. Whereas it is written in the holy canons of the fathers that the God-loving bishops in each administrative district ought to assemble together twice a year to deal with urgent matters that occur,[2] in due season we summon your love of God and urge you to come at once to us, and betake yourselves to the apostolic throne with the other saintly bishops, respecting matters that will assist and further the union of God's holy churches; which is a matter of concern and of earnest endeavour both to God himself and to our pious Christ-loving king. This we have made known p. 114.
to you all both individually and generally, and for this very same reason we have sent you so-and-so the devout reader of our apostolic see. *The end.*

[1] 2 Co. xiii. 5.

[2] Mansi ii. 669.

518-8. 35. *Of the same to Eustace the presbyter. (From those during episcopacy, from the 7th book the 140th, 142nd letter.)*

When I had read the letter of your love of God, I was desirous of carrying out what you ask and begging Jesus, who is God, to bestow the ordination of a deacon upon the devout brother John through my sinful and unworthy hand. But I was greatly opposed in this and my readiness hindered by the strictness of the canons, which do not on any other condition allow a man who has been afflicted with the yoke of slavery to enter the sacred clergy unless he has received manumission and removed from him the bond of slavery.[1] This principle was in fact observed by Peter who is among the saints, the bishop from Iberia, a man who in all things acted in accordance with the judgments of God. When father Timothy, an inmate of what is called the convent of Majuma, had been approved for admission to the presbyterate, he would not on any other condition allow him to receive ordination, unless those
p. 115. who were thought to be his masters had first bestowed freedom upon him: and then the God-loving presbyter father Theodore went with him and had the legal forms of manumission carried out in the church called that of Anthedon. For the monastery that is being built by your religiousness, and by help from God is on the

[1] Mansi i. 45.

point of being finished, we have sent you a very small present: which please receive contentedly: since the holy church here, having been laden with many debts by him who was ejected, does not allow me to show munificence or liberality even in urgent matters. Our common Christ-loving brother the lord Genesius we received with joy, and we offered him all that was in our power, seeing he is a man who deserves any trouble or effort. *The end.*

36. *Of the same to Eusebius the deacon at Apamea.* **513-7.**
(From those during episcopacy, from the 7th book the 218th letter.)

Those who bring you this letter came to us with the information that Libanius the devout presbyter, who is enrolled in the holy clergy at Apamea, wishes to exact interest from them as arising from a loan of his, contrary to the intention of the sacred canons. They say that they often entreated him to extend to them a hand of sympathy, and to be content with the amount **p. 116.**
of the principal [1] only, and they gained nothing. Be so good therefore as to remind this man through the religious *œconomi*, or stewards, and the devout archdeacon, or chief of the deacons, of the divine laws which say, "Thou shalt not exact interest from thy brother," [2] and "He giveth not his money upon

[1] κεφάλαιον.

[2] De. xxiii. 19 (?); Ex. xxii. 25 (?).

interest,"[1] and "Interest and guile departed not from her streets,"[2] and things like these. Following in the tracks of these texts, the God-clad instructors[3] of the church also forbade interest and usury to those who act as priests to God, fixing a fitting punishment and penalty for such unjust acquisition.[4] Put him therefore, the aforesaid devout presbyter Libanius, in memory of these things, and persuade him to do what beseems him and not to do despite either to his own spiritual office, or to God's laws. But let him yield to the kinship and consanguinity of nature, lest he call down upon himself the severity of the canons. For it is better for him to follow the divine counsel not of necessity but of his own will. *The end.*

p. 117.

513-7. 37. *Of the same to Simeon, bishop of Chalcis.* (*From those during episcopacy, from the 7th book the 238th, 240th letter.*)

The devout monk so-and-so came to us, sadly lamenting and saying that he had been separated by your love of God and forbidden to live in the monastery of the holy lord 'Akiba, where he had also been educated from the beginning and practised philosophic modes of life. What moved you to this was, he said, because it was he who told us that the man who is *chorepiscopus* and also *periodeutes* of the village of

[1] Ps. xiv. 5. [2] Ps. liv. 12. [3] *Marzane* = μύσται. [4] Mansi ii. 676.

Thelhadin, who had previously been tried by us at a time when the saintly bishops were here, and themselves also joined us in the examination, had treated the canonical inhibition with contempt and presumed to take part in the sacred ministry. When I learned this, I judged it right to send and tell your love of God that, as God is witness, I did not even know the very name of this monk, nor was I acquainted with his personal appearance, until I learned it[1] just now, when he made the complaint to me; nor was it he who disclosed a fact that was hidden: for it was already being whispered by everyone. Whence those of the house of the God-loving bishop Maron also had learned it before this came to the knowledge of my vileness, and they were distressed in themselves, and did not reveal p. 118.
it or tell it out: but they concealed the distress and kept it to themselves, as the truth is witness. It is therefore the duty of your love of God to release the man from his inhibition, seeing that it is without cause, and he gave no handle for blame against him. For the *chorepiscopus* or *periodeutes*, whom we just now mentioned, whether it is openly or secretly that he presumes to transgress the law by treating with contempt the inhibition from us, in the same way and without any difference rouses the wrath of God. For, though a man escape men's eyes, he cannot escape the eye that sees everything. Let such a man hear also from the singing prophet, "He that planted the ears,

[1] Masc., *i.e.* the name.

doth He not hear? or He that created the eyes, doth He not perceive?"[1] Let this therefore be a matter for inquiry, and for your consideration: for our part, bound as we are by respect for your venerable age, we commit everything to you: for I know that, as you have undergone a contest on behalf of the orthodox faith, and have shown great concern on behalf of accuracy in this respect, so you will show similar concern in the case of the canons. But for the present please release from his inhibition the devout monk whom we have many times mentioned, who brings you this letter; since, to say the truth, he has not committed any of
p. 119. the sins with which you have charged him. As to the matters[2] that were the cause of the devout deacon Stephen coming to you, do your diligence to handle them as befits you and is reasonable, in order that none of the troubles which have been stirred up may remain without healing and without cure. This will bring you no small praise both in the sight of God and in the sight of men. *The end.*

518-7. 38. *Of the same to the same Simeon, bishop of Chalcis.* (*From those during episcopacy, from the 7th book the 267th, 269th letter.*)

For my part I had no need of words and of assurance by letter as regards the various matters that have happened and been transacted with the tranquillity of

[1] Ps. xciii. 9.

[2] κεφάλαια.

your love of God, since the facts, if one may so say, utter a voice and plainly cry this out. But, because there is a time to speak, as there is also a time to keep silence, according to the saying of the wise Koholeth,[1] I now wish to repeat again as in a summary[2] the events that occurred before, and to say like the prophet, "I have kept silence, lest I should keep silence also for ever; I have refrained myself like a travailing woman."[3] Your holiness probably, I think, remembers that all through the summer the men from the village called Thelhadin were urging us, p. 120.
and that, though their request was refused by us once and twice (I do not hesitate to say even three times and many times), so that a chance might be given you of settling their affair by some wise method and God-pleasing plan, we effected nothing at all, but we were more pressingly and more violently urged by them, and we were now being abused even by the citizens themselves who saw that they were continually complaining to us and did not receive any answer; and thenceforward we had also to submit to murmurs of no ordinary kind. Whence also we exhorted the devout presbyter Ignatius, who happened to be here, to appease the men by some means and invite them to a peaceful frame of mind. At last, not to make a long story, we were compelled to resort to such an extreme measure as bringing the *periodeutes* himself here and having the details of the case[4] examined before the

[1] Ec. iii. 7 [2] κεφάλαιον. [3] Is. xlii. 14. [4] ὑπόθεσις.

saintly bishops. How repulsive to the ears the counts[1] of the accusations that were examined were I forbear to state, seeing that the gravity of these is known to those who examined them with us, and closed their ears when they were being examined and proved. But this I know clearly, that in the middle of the examination into these things the same *periodeutes* wanted to run away; and in the hearing
p. 121. of everyone and while he was standing up I said to him in clear and distinct tones, directing the words towards him, "If you dare to depart, you old man, before the investigation is ended, you will be excommunicate, and under deprivation." Upon hearing this he promised not to run away. And the next day, when his presence was required, though he was sitting in what is called the *psepheion*, and had been seen by certain men, he would not come: but he formed the plan of running away, and departed while in full health, thus offending against the reverence due to the apostolic see, and against the synod of saintly bishops. The saintly bishops Sergius and Marion, who are much devoted to your love of God, are trustworthy witnesses of these things. These things therefore having thus passed in order and been transacted, it is now your part, not mine, to say what punishment the man deserves who presumed to take part in priestly functions and down to yesterday to write letters as a *chorepiscopus* and to administer the affairs of the

[1] κεφάλαια.

district. When a man dares even to lie and swear, and to retain a thing in ignorance, and that after he has personally received the prohibition, what chance of forgiveness or indulgence can he have? Who is there even among men of very peaceful disposition whom he is not treating as a fool and rousing to an anger that is just and well-pleasing to God? For for a man to be jealous for the divine laws when they are p. 122.
transgressed is to offer a sacrifice to God, just as the opposite course, I mean to be silent on such occasions, is to rouse the wrath of Him who laid down such laws. And yet we for the sake of your holiness' tranquillity remained silent, as we ought not to have done under such circumstances: and, when at an earlier time those who came from the monastery of the holy lord 'Akiba were asking us about the same said *chorepiscopus* or *periodeutes*, we kept silence out of respect to you, because we were ashamed to expose the abominable character of the affair, of which even men of no distinction were not unaware. Quite recently again, when the religious presbyter father Cosmas came to us about this same matter, and said that his conscience and that of the others was wounded, and that they ought not to communicate with a man who had trampled upon the strictness of the canons, and had reckoned the ban of excommunication as nothing, we were compelled to tell them the whole affair, and to place the facts proved by examination before their eyes and read them to them, fearing as we did the prophetic curse which lays under a miserable con-

demnation those who call bitter sweet or darkness light.[1] After this again the letter of your love of God came, and we gathered together in our mind all the details of the same affair, and we summoned the said
p. 123. God-loving presbyter Cosmas to us, and we had some conversation with him concerning peace and concord; after which we thought it right for the sake of your holiness' tranquillity to relieve the above-mentioned presbyter from his punishment, and allow him communion: but only on condition of his remaining quiet and not approaching the office of *chorepiscopus* or *periodeutes* in any way, because, to speak in the words of scripture and in fitting language, some had been caused to stumble through him.[2] But, while I was in the middle of writing these things, the company of the men of Thelhadin again assailed me, buzzing about my ears like bees: and they were again dismissed by us with insult and with many contumelies heaped upon them. It is therefore the duty of your sanctity to appoint such a *chorepiscopus* and *periodeutes* for them that God may be praised, and all occasion be cut off from those that wish to find occasion. *The end.*

513-7. 39. *Of the same to the clergy and notables of Apamea.* (*From those during episcopacy, from the 7th book the 289th letter.*)

The name and fact of concord is pleasing even in God's sight, for He himself said in the Gospel, "If

[1] Is. v. 20. [2] Mt. xiii 57.

two of you shall agree on earth touching any matter whatsoever they shall ask, it shall be done for them by my Father which is in heaven";[1] and in the statute p. 124.
of piety also concerning the nomination of bishops it is ordained that a deliberate vote upon this must by all means be put forward by the common consent of the religious clergymen and of the eloquent and illustrious notables; a principle which our pious Christ-loving king also ratified.[2] Wherefore we urge you again, as we have also already done,[3] and that many times, to come to a united election of him to whom the bishopric of the illustrious metropolis of the Apamenes is to be entrusted. When you were divided, we, who were not under the influence of passion, were obliged ourselves to choose by a judgment that did not respect persons and to nominate for you the devout presbyter Cosmas, a man who was reputed to be fitted for this, according to the prevailing opinion of many respecting him. But, considering also the greatness of the thing, he would not consent. And therefore I have determined again to urge you, as I have said, to a united vote, since those whom some of you chose by name did not seem to us to be fit men: and to send this letter to you the religious clergymen, and to the eloquent and magnificent *ktetores* and to the men of repute at the same time, in order that I may be the first to give you an example
of concord by not writing to you separately, but as to p. 125.

[1] Mt. xviii. 19. [2] C.J. I. iv. 17 (?). [3] i. 30.

one church which is the body of the one and only and undivided Christ. You will agree, I know well, if, free from all prejudice and cavilling and favour, and from other such influences, you will put in your *psephisma* three men who are in the first place sound in the orthodox faith and show this by holding firmly to communion with us, and secondly are in character free from avarice, and will not approach the high-priesthood with unwashen feet, as it is said, but men who have been trained, if only to a moderate degree, in exercises of virtue, and able to rule, and who besides humility possess also a practised intelligence, in order that they may rather rule those that are under their authority, and not themselves be ruled by them, but also be men practised in divine doctrines. For he who stands at the head must also be a man "apt to teach," and one who in character and speech shows himself "a pattern of good works," as the Apostle says.[1] For we have in fact no other reason for using strict language about such things except to avoid straying from what is right, and becoming liable to endless torment. For it is manifest that, although
p. 126. we are sinners, yet still in the nomination of bishops we in no point fall short of the principles about which many concern themselves. *The end.*

[1] 1 Ti. iii. 2; Tit. ii. 7.

40. *Of the same to Hypatius the Master of the Soldiers.*[1] *(From those during episcopacy, from the 7th book the 458th, 465th letter.)* 515-8.

Your excellency's exalted letters I for my part receive with all affection and pleasure. Though you are so exalted and have so much glory, to which the Lord brought you, you encourage even humble men like me to inform you of things that are the truth, since you place nothing before this. Wherefore I also will truthfully inform your highness of the reason for which I have now composed this mean letter. It was not the devout presbyter Julian only who was accused by the holy church of the Tarsians of detaining property that belonged of right to it, but many others also with him; and in connexion with such accusations those who made the charge and those who were under the charge often wished to have recourse to the apostolic throne of the city that belongs to the Antiochenes and to you. And, since it is my habit not to cause trouble to anyone, but as far as possible to remove the complications arising from affairs, and not to inflict the p. 127.
burden of heavy expense upon men who are compelled to take so long a journey, and at such grievous cost to discuss the points on which they are in doubt, I determined that all the saintly bishops of First Cilicia should sit in conjunction with the eloquent

[1] στρατηλάτης.

scholastics whom I certainly knew to be of good reputation, and who are well reported of both now and from their former life in Berytus, and discuss the details of the case of each of the persons who are said to be devouring church property. I also provided that two religious presbyters of the apostolic see, men versed in affairs and of minute experience in such matters, should be associated with them in the hearing of the said questions, with the book of the revered and holy gospels also laid in the midst. And after every point had been discussed in due order, and each of them had accepted the judgments given (how could they do otherwise?), the devout Julian only, being afflicted with covetousness, dared to treat the verdict[1] of the bishops with contempt contrary to the canons and the intention of the rightly-enacted laws, and to drag the hearing before a civil court, in so much as to incur indignation and the punishment prescribed by the canons. And upon his brother the God-
p. 128. loving Syrian, bishop of the city of Augusta, using many entreaties and promising to induce him to keep quiet his punishment was remitted, since I am in fact naturally inclined to the milder course. Indeed he tried by the use of deception to make the illustrious Heliodorus your *curator* also an accomplice in his plot by giving him false information : and upon your highness obtaining previous information of his proceedings all his plan was shattered. And now again, as if

[1] ἀπόφασις.

dealing with a new matter he has set himself to entreat your highness, and to seem to be making a moderate request, that he may plead his cause before civil magistrates, after the examination and decision of the apostolic see and of the whole synod, the reversal of a decision of which is not permitted him by any authority, either by the holy canons or by the civil laws. Therefore by his words which are moderate and have a supplicatory appearance he is trying by means of his tricks to suppress things which have passed in order and been brought to a conclusion in this way. And his thoughts are, as one of the prophets said, "a pondering of iniquity, and his sin is hid."[1] For how did he expect to get anything of this kind from you who are very just, seeing that everyone who has made havoc of the property of the church would have imitated his example, and reversed judgments rightly given, and transferred ecclesiastical causes[2] to a magisterial tribunal, and that after judg- p. 129.
ment had been given and they had received an ending consonant to the laws and to the intention of the divine canons? Therefore I beg and entreat your excellency not to give him an opportunity of appealing to your friendship, and arming himself against the ordinances of the holy church, and destroying all discipline, of which you both are and ever will be a guardian and a protector, so long as you are preserved through your whole life. *The end.*

[1] Ho. xiii. 12.

[2] ὑποθέσεις.

513-8. 41. *Of the same to Solon the bishop.* (*From those during episcopacy, from the 7th book the 51st, 42nd letter.*)

It is written somewhere in the legal writings that the divine Moses, after appointing judges over Israel, allowed them to judge unimportant causes (I must quote the actual expression of the God-inspired utterances):[1] but a hard matter they were to report to him, and from him to receive the solution that God "the knower of secrets" (this also I take from another scripture)[2] should reveal and signify to him. You also therefore as a giver and teacher of divine laws have followed this rule and reported to the apostolic see (not to my mean self who scarcely see even what
p. 130. is before my feet owing to the denseness of my understanding) a matter which seemed to be hard. Therefore your love of God must know that Maximus the presbyter, who has fallen into the snare of fornication, although he has shown fervent repentance, and for a period of five years has given himself up to such labours, cannot be restored and take his place in the sacred office: and it is a simple thing for us to obtain a solution of this question without trouble from the holy canons themselves. For indeed the God-loving bishops who met together at Neocæsarea made these distinct pronouncements in the ninth canon: "If a

[1] Ex. xviii. 26. [2] Su. 42.

presbyter be promoted after having previously sinned with his body, and confess that he sinned before ordination, he shall not offer: but he shall retain the rest of his functions on account of his zeal in other respects."[1] If then a man who before ordination has sinned with his body, *i.e.* has committed fornication (for this the Apostle also said, "Every sin is without the body, but he that committeth fornication sinneth against his own body"[2]), is not permitted to offer, but to retain the rest of his functions on account of his zeal in other respects, how can it be doubted that he who has committed this same sin after ordination cannot offer the divine sacrifice, or consecrate the water of regeneration, or perform any such function? p. 131.
Let no man say, "What then is the advantage of repentance to a man who has committed fornication, if he is not after labours of continence to be restored to the sacred service?" Repentance brings about forgiveness and bestows communion in the bloodless sacrifice for the sake of purification and preservation upon those who wash away the sin by tears and the other forms of bodily mortification: but the service of the priesthood is the reward of a blameless character. The ninth canon of the three hundred and eighteen holy fathers also says thus, as you also know, "If men have without examination been promoted to be presbyters, and[3] being examined have confessed the sins committed by them, and after they have confessed

[1] Mansi ii. 542. [2] 1 Co. vi. 18. [3] Gk. ἤ.

some men being moved in a manner contrary to the canon have laid a hand upon them, such men the canon does not accept: for the catholic church requires blamelessness."[1] I forbear to say that you have adopted a very mild policy and one of exceeding leniency in the matter of Maximus, because the canon did not say anything plainly about a man who commits fornication after ordination. You have openly permitted him (this was stated in your letter) to perform evening and morning prayers, and to sit on every
p. 132. occasion with the presbyters, a thing forbidden in the case of a man who has sinned before ordination and afterwards confessed; for this is clearly written down in the ninth canon of those who met together at Neocæsarea, which we mentioned a short time ago, which says that he should retain the rest of his functions on account of his zeal in other respects, but should not again go so far as to offer the rational sacrifice, and do things like this and of equal honour. Therefore, since you have the nature of what ought to be done from the canonical utterances themselves, do not allow anyone to take refuge in the unknown, and in the pretence of searching into the spirit of the holy canons. One seeks for the spirit in cases where nothing is defined in actual words and phrases.[2] *The end.*

[1] Mansi ii. 672. [2] λέξεις.

42. *Of the same to the fathers.* (*From those during episcopacy, from the 4th book the 64th letter.*) 518-7.

Of the circumstances in which we are placed I notified your holinesses before when I sent the letter through the holy monastery at Aphthoria.[1] If you have received this letter, please let me know this by a missive of your own.

And after other things. But Philip, the devout monk from Isauria, who was ordained deacon by me, deceived by avaricious thoughts, in truth yielded to p. 133. some deceivers and conceived the idea of digging and bringing up treasure. And he incurred blame from me on this account, and was expelled from the chapel of the forty holy martyrs, and was ordered to visit himself with labours of repentance. If therefore he is living in the holy monastery of father Romanus of holy memory, you are acting rightly in allowing him to communicate in the oblation, but excluding him from the deacons' ministry, until he shows fruits of repentance for a certain period of time. As to him who holds the prelacy of the city of the men of Jerusalem,[2] no news has reached us personally as to his reconciliation. But that the man is utterly unstable and weak, seeing that from the very beginning he has lived such a confused and inconstant life, and has thus been raised to the position that he now holds, all who know

[1] Near Cæsarea in Palestine (vit. Pet. Ib. p. 120). [2] *Cf.* p. 129.

him are well aware, and I have no need of words on this point. I was glad to see the God-loving presbyter father Apaphon, as I said before, and I thought the man's coming a great blessing, and you may be sure that I would have bought this at a high price; and I have incurred a debt of thanks to Christ our Saviour and God in that I received this pleasure for nothing through your saintly prayers. The sum of gold that was spent by him upon the well, I mean the sum of
p. 134. fifty darics, we paid to him out of a certain God-loving loan. For, believe me, we have not a *mina*: and this is the only way in which we are relieved in poverty: while in our other pursuits we distress God and do nothing at all that is pleasing to Him. *The end.*

513-8. 43. *Of the same to the archimandrite of the monastery of the holy lord Simeon.* (*From those during episcopacy, from the 8th book the 134th letter.*)

Whereas Nonnus even before entering the holy Simeon's flock was often summoned to answer the charges and accusations that were being brought against him and did not obey, but, even when placed under an injunction by the God-loving *ekklesiekdikoi*, trampled upon this with similar impudence, like a man who had grown accustomed to treat holy things with contempt, and after repairing to me by night once only and in secret, as if doing things worthy of night and darkness, thought that he had thus done enough to give satisfaction (?), and at last after receiving an explicit letter through your religiousness continued in the same shameless state, I for my part endured, and was not roused to just indignation: but after appointing him a limit[1] of ten days I allowed him to have this doubled. And he behaved exactly as one who had not been summoned, alleging only pretexts founded upon sins, and answered through your religiousness that he asked that clergymen should not be present at his trial, because they are clergymen who have been injured by him, and from whom he used to receive the unhallowed and profane gains. For he did the same as those who have stolen or committed adultery, or perpetrated a murder, and say that those who have been outraged and injured by theft and those who have thus suffered by adultery and those who have suffered by murder ought not to be present at their trial. No wonder if, being guilty of such evil deeds, he belches forth such words. What will they say who "hate judgment and pervert all right things, and build Zion with blood and Jerusalem with iniquity,"[2] as one of the prophets somewhere said? For how can one help saying that the hands are full of blood which have sold the gifts of the Holy Spirit, which he had no right to give to some men, or to take away from those who possess them? For this is the wonderful point about his sacrilege, that he used to hide himself as in some lurking place, I mean in hypocrisy, while hearing at

p. 135.

[1] προθεσμία.

[2] Mi. iii. 9, 10.

p. 136. every ordination the anathemas and terrific curses that I pronounced against such unlawful gains, and to stop his ears "like the deaf asp that stoppeth her ears, which will not hearken to the voice of the charmer,"[1] as the singing prophet says. However, that I may not by using many words protract the letter unnecessarily, this is the second and third summons that I am addressing to him through your love of God, or, rather to speak more truly, a summons that has the force of the tenth and twentieth (for one may justly reckon them as equal in number to the days that have passed); since I wish even if late yet some time or other to induce him to make a defence, with the saintly bishops present according to the intention of the holy canons, and ready to conduct his trial, with the holy Gospels laid in the midst, and the terrific threat pronounced by them hanging over those who turn aside justice.[2] But, if even after this letter he shall dare to delay, then after this the same divine statutes of church discipline shall pronounce judgment and the fitting verdict[3] upon him. For we for our part in no way wished the circumstances of his case to remain unknown to the glorious notables also in Antiochus' city: but we even brought these as far as was possible to their knowledge; and we would have urged them and some of the
p. 137. learned rhetors to be judges of the cause,[4] had it not been that we were hindered by reflecting upon the order of the holy canons, which command that ecclesi-

[1] Ps. lvii. 5, 6. [2] Lu. xiii. 27 (?). [3] ἀπόφασις. [4] ὑπόθεσις.

astical cases shall be tried and decided by saintly bishops,[1] and subject to penalties those who pass over these and turn to civil courts.[2] And it was for this same reason that we sent the religious Eusebius the deacon also; for we cannot consent, after the lapse of so many days, to keep the saintly bishops here, when they ought to return to their own flock. *The end.*

44. *Of the same to Eutychian, governor of Apamea.* **514–8.**
(From those during episcopacy, from the 8th book the 190th letter.)

When I compare the reports that have recently come to my hearing with the words spoken by your magnificence when I was leaving the royal city and had reached this city of Antiochus, I still even now consider these untrustworthy and shrink from setting them down in so many words in this letter. I learn that, when one of those who have been deprived and p. 138.
stripped of the high-priestly office was celebrating (as he thinks) the unhallowed memory of martyrs and the initiatory festival and dedication of a certain house, you also went there and took part in a feast that thus contends against God. In order that you may not think that it is from a quarrelsome disposition that we have been led to use such hard words, or rather in order that you may know that what I have written

[1] *Cf.* Mansi vii. 361.
[2] δικαστήρια.

falls short of the real abomination, I will immediately quote to you the actual canon and law of the Spirit, and you will know clearly that for a man who is in servitude to the pious king and is the ruler of a people to do anything of the kind without consideration is not a thing free from danger. The canon or law that has been mentioned is as follows:—"If any bishop, after he has been deprived by a synod, or a presbyter or deacon by his bishop, shall presume to perform any part of the ministry, be he a bishop according to the previously existing custom, or a presbyter or deacon, no hope of restoration even in another synod shall thenceforward be permitted him, nor shall he be permitted an opportunity of defence: but those also who communicate with him shall all be expelled from
p. 139. the church, and especially if they have presumed to communicate with the aforesaid persons after they have learned the verdict that has been put forth against them."[1] Do you think even after reading this law that it is about small or contemptible matters that we are speaking; or that we do so out of concern for your soul and for your reputation?[2] You must therefore abandon this discreditable state of mind, if indeed it really is a state of mind at all, and reflect upon the purpose of God and of our pious king, and of the glorious notables who are earnest upholders of the orthodox faith, and not set yourself in hostility to the saintly Peter bishop of your metropolis in any-

[1] Mansi ii. 1309.

[2] ὑπόληψις.

thing, or rather not conceive any thought that is hostile and hateful to God, and to our triumphant, serene, Christ-loving king. *The end.*

45. *Of the same to Conon the brigand-chaser.* (*From those during episcopacy, from the 8th book the 237th letter.*) 513-8.

Concerning the unholy woman who in an unhallowed manner thrust herself into the degree of the diaconate I both wrote to your magnificence before, and am now again writing, though I ascribe the whole affair to an evil demon and to my sins, not to you. However, p. 140.
since much contumely is being poured upon me, and for the sake of the blamelessness of ecclesiastical order, and to preserve mere holiness itself, the object of veneration, I legally placed the hateful and all-presumptuous woman under deprivation, stripping her of the supposed office; and she was convicted and even herself confessed that she had been married three times, her third husband being still alive. Therefore you for your part ought not to have recorded against yourself a thing that has been once condoned by me: but you should have been glad and have known clearly that we for our part love you sincerely, and hold you in all veneration and respect. In another letter also I made known to your greatness that the glorious patrician and lieutenant of the Master of the Soldiers[1]

[1] στρατηλάτης; *cf.* p. 60.

in the East excellent in all good qualities has composed a letter to you which has the force of a command, in which he gives you leave to support the orthodox and the interests of the church with ample freedom and liberty. To speak plainly, in order not to make a long story, you have abundant warrant for displaying your qualities against God's enemies. *The end.*

p. 141.

513-8. 46. *Of the same to the clergymen of Antaradus.* (*From those during episcopacy, from the 8th book the 264th, 265th letter.*)

When I had read your devoutnesses' petitions concerning the necessity of a shepherd being nominated for you,[1] in accordance with the precepts of the holy canons and the laws of the Spirit, and concerning the articles that belong of right to your holy church, but are unreasonably and unjustly detained by others, after giving due consideration to the whole matter I thought it right to refer the whole case[2] to our serene Christ-loving king and his pious ears. For it is from him after God that we receive useful and satisfactory assistance in difficult affairs. Wherefore it is your duty at once to insert in a *psephisma* three men well-known for virtue and capable of being entrusted with a rational leadership of this kind, in order that we may choose the man who stands highest in these respects, and confer

[1] *Cf.* Mansi viii. 1075.

[2] ὑπόθεσις.

ordination upon him; or rather present him for the inspiration of the Spirit: for the choice and judgment and bestowal in such matters are from above: since in fact "every good bestowal and every perfect gift is from above, coming down from the Father of lights,"[1] as the sacred scripture somewhere says. Let this be both considered and performed in this way, and may it be brought to a good end by God! Whereas the devout deacon Stephen has just presented petitions to me and informed me that Leontius, who has lived an p. 142.
unhallowed life, but was improperly admitted to ordination as deacon, as if setting himself to act in accordance with his former life, contracted a second marriage after ordination, and after this was by the bishop's judgment struck out of the sacred tablets, and as an indulgence was allowed to minister again, but now wishes to retain deacon's rank and claims to be made head over the others, though he ought not to be ranked even among those that are under a head, how can we neglect the intimation that has been given us, and close our ears to such audacious deeds on his part? Even if it is the case that, while your holy church was without anyone to act as shepherd, the man who then held the post of archdeacon by a presumptuous action enrolled him in the order of deacons, this action is already in every way invalid. This man ought therefore to stand entirely outside the ministry, and to feel the sins that he has committed, and to congratulate himself that he does not gain

[1] Ja. i. 17.

experience of some canonical punishment; not go on further to desire the headship that it is no way proper for him to hold. But the first position in the order of religious deacons shall be held by those who are summoned from among the members of the order. For the present this is the conclusion at which we have arrived: but, if Leontius thinks that he has any right
p. 143. founded upon the canons that may help him, let him inform the apostolic see of this; and the fact of the accusation will not do him any harm whatever, if he have truth on his side. If he was conscious of guilt even on one count[1] only of those that were related to us, he ought, he ought indeed to have restricted himself to a modest and humble demeanour, and thought of Him who said by Jeremiah the prophet, "'Hear these things, foolish people and without understanding, which have eyes and see not, and have ears and hear not! or will ye not fear me,' saith the Lord, 'and will ye not tremble at my face, which have placed the sand as a bound for the sea, an everlasting decree, and it shall not pass it?'"[2] However for our part we feared for his sake owing to the terrible nature of the reports, and were unable to remain silent in such circumstances. And, since the church ministry "requires blamelessness,"[3] we decided that he should cease to exercise this, in order that we might not seem even to ourselves by acquiescing in the sins that he committed and the deeds that he thought good to do, to be by our silence actually

[1] κεφάλαιον. [2] Jer. v. 21, 22. [3] Mansi ii. 672.

approving the evil thing, and apply to ourselves the words spoken by God to the same prophet, "A wonder and a horror has happened upon the earth; the prophets prophesy falsehood, and the priests clapped their hands."[1]

But, since we are always desirous of arriving at the truth, and we know that the magnificent Christ-loving count John is very desirous of this, we have written to his magnificence to examine into the true state of the case, and notify our meanness of it. For in everything let truth and justice be respected; while at the same time the honour of the holy church is preserved, and the ministry has the reverence assigned to it which is its by right, especially by those to whom this ministry p. 144.
has been committed, through the benignance and ineffable grace of God. *The end.*

47. *Of the same to Cassian bishop of Bostra.* (*From those during episcopacy, from the 8th book the 288th letter.*) 518-7.

It is nothing surprising if the prelate of the city of the men of Jerusalem,[2] being such in his character and in his faith as everyone knows him to be, but as I for my part loathe even to take upon my lips, has done this act also which you have mentioned in violation of the holy canons, I mean the act of raising to the bishopric a man who was included in

[1] Jer. v. 31.

[2] *Cf.* p. 119.

the clergy of your holy church. On the contrary one ought to have been surprised if one such as he in his faith and in his character had done anything canonical and according to regulation. We have told this therefore to those who manage our *apokriseis* in the royal city.

As to Agapius the devout bishop, we have this much to say, that, if the offences committed by him are of such a nature, this man must be corrected by canonical reproofs: with moderation however on account of the difficulty of the time, and because the man has now "grown old in evil days," as the sacred scripture says,[1] and has already come near to being reckoned with those that are in Hades. For "God is
p. 145. faithful, who will not suffer"[2] those that are not rightly disposed towards Him to outrage the sacred prelacy for a great length of time, so that through them His name should be "blasphemed among the nations," as it is written.[3] *The end.*

513-7. 48. *Of the same to Philoxenus bishop of Hierapolis. (From those during episcopacy, from the* 10*th book the* 295*th letter.)*

Hearing the divine writings which say, "Salvation cometh by much counsel,"[4] I wish yet now again to ask your sanctity even about a matter upon which we have often already counselled and deliberated. You

[1] Su. 52. [2] 1 Co. x. 13. [3] Ro. ii. 24. [4] Pr. xxiv. 6.

know that those who received ordination for payment and bought for themselves from Flavian the trafficker in all divine things the grace of the Spirit that is not to be bought, alleging ignorance of the strictness of the holy canons, begged you and the other bishops of the other resplendent metropolitan cities that they might obtain forgiveness on the ground of ignorance of the sin. And, though the same said men further brought us letters written in lenient terms from one and another set of persons, even so they did not obtain release from the interdicts. And some of them even went up to the royal city, and showed letters of this kind to those who conduct our *apokriseis* and to all p. 146.
those who are in power and deign to love our meanness, and caused them all, though certainly in a friendly manner, to charge me with cruelty. For all being moved to pity for them granted them forgiveness. And, when they returned thence, they did not desist from this course of action, since we even after this would not incline our ear to their entreaty and lamentation: but they went to the holy cloisters of the orthodox and moved the chiefs or rulers of the solitary and sacred orders to compassion. And they also, after weeping for the fall of certain persons, in an exactly similar manner and much more earnestly than the others, addressed supplications to us in writing with the object of procuring for them liberation from their evil plight. Being in some sort harassed and troubled by all the facts stated, I have taken the course of asking your holiness by this letter whether

these men ought to receive forgiveness at the feast of the Epiphany or if they ought not, let your love of God put yourself to a little trouble, and after the feast mentioned repair to this great Christ-loving city of Antiochus, and assist in a course of lenient mildness towards men who have sinned from ignorance, a course perhaps not wholly inconsistent with canonical strictness : for they say that the gift was concealed under the name of a present by those gain-hunters, and it deceived them. *The end.*

p. 147.

519-20. 49. *Of the same to John and John presbyters and archimandrites and the rest. (From those after banishment, from the 1st book the 55th, 53rd letter.)*

I am glad and rejoice greatly whenever I write an epistle to your holinesses, and, if one may so say, fancy myself speaking to you as if you were close by me. *And after other things.* For do not think of me that my concern for the church of the Alexandrines is different from my concern for that of the Antiochenes ; I shall not be lying even though I say it is much greater. In fact both the party of the learned Hippocrates, to whom I referred a short time ago, and a very large number of other well-known and distinguished men, who have always concerned themselves about their own salvation and about the strict observance of the orthodox faith, and those who followed these, through the efforts and endeavours

(to speak with God's permission) of my wretched miserable self joined the catholic and orthodox church in Egypt; men who as you know for a long time had not communicated, but were satisfied by the minutes[1] of the records[2] drawn up by the blessed Dioscorus who a short time ago departed to God, of which you no doubt have an *ison* or copy, and are not ignorant of the purport of the things contained in them: since, after the sacred old man had received the epistle p. 148.
written by my meanness, in answer to his synodical letter, with hands and feet, as the saying goes, and as far as was possible he complied with my advice and satisfied those who were separated; who often wrote to me in their letters (although it is in folly that I speak), "It is because we have confidence in your reputation[3] that we have communicated." How then can I neglect such men? or how can it be said that I must not both "in season and out of season" as the divine Apostle says[4] search even into small matters, and cut away every cause of stumbling, and remove the stones and cast them out [of] the way that leads . . .

. . . .

or to satisfy so-and-so and so-and-so individually, so that all these and men like them were scandalized in that a door for vain speaking was being opened to the contentious. For neither are this time and that alike, nor yet can you on your part avoid doing everything in the capacity of my representatives. For, what you do,

---

[1] πρᾶξις. [2] ὑπομνήματα. [3] ὑπόληψις. [4] 2 Ti. iv. 2.

that men will justly reckon to me; for all, both brothers and strangers, both friends and enemies, know clearly that I and you are one, as in fact we are. Accordingly, if any man owing to his imperfect
p. 149. intelligence needs to be directed by pilotage, being carried about like some ship by troubled thoughts, let him be so directed and controlled as not to rouse any storm or tempest against the great ships. Let not your sanctities think that this is the first time that I have been moved to this action. Even while I was living in Antiochus' city, I used to hear it said of the presbyter father Theodore of saintly memory that, when many came to Egypt and asked him whether they ought to communicate, he would answer and say plainly to them, "If you have been satisfied, communicate": and other things that are like this and resemble it. And I endured because it was a time of endurance, and because none of the bishops in the East heard anything of the kind, but the reports were confined to yourselves, and did no great harm. For a man who is doing anything in accordance with God's purpose never halts and hesitates in his action: but he stands firm and steadfast, and increases what he has begun, like the gift of the talents in the gospels.

And after other things. As to the devout and beloved brother Epimachus, you know how distinct the apostolic statute is through which I also was prevented from laying my hands upon this man, when he came to Antiochus' city, in order that he might conduct
p. 150. my *apokriseis* in the royal among cities, in conjunction

with the presbyter Peter of blessed memory, my brother. And, being afraid of the strictness of the canon, I restrained my desire: and this though I loved the man, I mean the devout Epimachus, not out of human favour, but on account of his devout and modest conduct in the monastic life, and his venerable age and old-fashioned mind. For I saw that the canon of the church everywhere "requires blamelessness";[1] and at the same time also I was in the habit of proclaiming to everyone in Antiochus' city, "No man who has been twice married or labours under any disqualification similar [to this] can [receive] ordination from me." . . . .

. . . .

Therefore take the course of which our Lord shall satisfy you." Accordingly it would not have been right for us, when the thing has been made public, to advance him now to ordination, and let him be a blot in our ministry, as the very wise Paul says,[2] us who endeavour with God's help to do everything as far as we can without cause for blame. For we cannot in fact say that the man by his monastic habit and the long life that he has passed in this is able to mitigate the strictness of the canon, seeing that it nowhere in actual words makes any such further provision about the twice-married, and seeing that "what is rare is not a law of the church," as the Theologian Gregory somewhere says.[3] The ninth canon of the three hundred and p. 151.

[1] Mansi ii. 672. [2] 2 Co. vi. 3. [3] Or. xxxix. 14.

eighteen holy fathers also plainly says that presbyters who have been put forward without examination shall be set aside, even though it is after ordination that their sin which violates the canon is confessed.[1] The twice-married have also a certain definite time provided in the same canons, during which they are excluded from communion,[2] because these men ought to devote themselves to fastings and prayers. Hence it is very plain that devout conduct after the second marriage is of assistance to them only in the way of penitence, and does not besides this also assist them in obtaining admission to the clergy. We know also the letter written by the saintly archbishop and martyr Dioscorus concerning Irenæus the twice-married, and the order of Theodosius of truly pious and God-loving memory concerning this man.[3] These things then being so, it rests with you and with those who disputed with you to consider whether one can extend the application of the fifty-third canon and compel it to cover the case of a man who, having contracted a second marriage, is ordained without examination, and to come to an agreement with one another on this point and settle your dispute and doubt. The canon itself is as follows: "If a presbyter be promoted after having previously sinned with his body, and confess that he
p. 152. sinned before ordination, he shall not offer: but he shall retain the rest of his functions on account of his zeal in other respects. For in the case of other sins

[1] Mansi, *l.c.* [2] *Ibid.*, 563.; Bas. Ep. 188. 4. [3] Mansi v. 420.

many have said that they are remitted by the mere fact of the laying on of hands. But, if he do not himself confess, and it is not possible for him to be manifestly convicted, the discretion shall rest with himself."[1] Consider therefore whether the devout Epimachus also ought to communicate in the prayers and other things only. But even this I say as an indulgence, not as a command. For the principles laid down by the canon do not refer to an open and notorious second marriage, but to other bodily sins that are secret. But for your part, since it is upon you that the burden of judgment is laid, choose the course that seems to you good: my feebleness cannot write about this: in fact for my part whatever I have given if I have given anything I have given for your sakes as the representative of Christ. However it is with much sorrow and sighing that I have written this (I speak with God as witness), seeing that even to the devout Epimachus himself that which is thought an honour is being turned into a shame, and I too am being driven by the divine precepts to break out into grievous and bitter words. For what we are to say upon the point in question is laid down for us as a law by others. There is another thing that, as upon brief consideration appears to my meanness, would have been just and proper, I mean if you had asked me first and taken my advice, especially since it is now a kind of beginning of our state[2] of banishment. You are not unaware that in p. 153.

[1] *Id.*, ii. 542. [2] κατάστασις.

the case of the man of holy memory also, I mean Peter the bishop, even when he was not ordaining anyone, those who were ordaining took his advice. Timothy too, who bravely endured in the contests of piety, when he was at a distance and was living somewhere far away beyond the boundaries, used to regulate all these things by epistle, and they were carried into effect. However you may allege in defence that I was in hiding and that you did not even know where I am, and that you were in a hurry to satisfy your need, which it would not have been certainly possible to do when you wanted. Another matter, I confess, was very displeasing to me, I mean the fact that certain other men also who rejoice in two disciples only, and those boys, have presented those who are living with them for ordination, so that they are led astray from the very fact of living with them. For a boy who is admitted to an honour which passes his measure exposes himself to shame, while he has for the time brought no small blame on the community.

Your remark that the God-loving Isidore the bishop ought not on account of the persecution to have again laid his hand on those who were ordained deacons by me is lukewarm and cold : for these regulations apply to deacons enrolled in the churches: and to monasteries round about that parish. But to extend this to those
p. 154. who are in a province[1] beyond the boundaries and are united with us in respect of the right faith it is not

[1] ἐπαρχία.

a fitting season. In the same fashion also the practice of devout women living in their houses being ordained deaconesses is very usual and is diffused, if I may so say, over the whole world.

Again the fact that in previous times Palestine also was subject to the apostolic see of the city of the Antiochenes is in no doubt. However I and the God-loving bishop Isidore make up one person, and I myself say that his love of God performed the ordination on my behalf; therefore let all question and dispute cease. The quality of the person who ordained causes no detriment whatever, such that the ordination that has been performed should be thought to be uncanonical. But you, who are wise in the Lord, ought not to have dropped the religious presbyter Victor out of your consideration: seeing[1] that he would often introduce some useful action before the event itself, or that after consenting to what you did he was thenceforward ashamed to go against his own consent; and seeing[1] that many find it hard to endure neglect. But that he was your friend not only I but everyone is aware. I know, I know clearly that it was with judgment that you put forward your devout brothers: but the reason that you yielded to certain men who were putting forward boys was, as it seems, that you might not excite disturbance against you. These things I have written to you by

[1] Or "on the ground": there is perhaps some corruption in this sentence.

p. 155. way of admonition, and privately. For indeed I know how to admonish such men as you, but to find fault with those who are so exalted in virtue I have not learned, far less to rebuke them, as you write. I know my measure, even though the fact of the office and the spiritual honour that has been given me through the benignance of God tends to exaltation, a thing that to the unintelligent and foolish gives occasion for vanity and pride, but in those who do not deceive themselves and know that they are sinners implants endurance in contests and fear of the judgment, in which we shall give account even for honours that are so high, when the Judge shall give judgment, as is threatened in the prophets, against those that are "clothed in other men's apparel." [1] *Not the end.*

519-20. 50. *Of the same to the same John and John presbyters and archimandrites and the rest.* (*From those after banishment, from the first book the* 16*th letter.*)

If those who were enlightened in their understanding like you, and for this reason were properly called seers, were a cause of peace to others also by giving the inner man peace from warring passions, and heard from those who approached them the words, "Thy coming, seer, is peace," [2] what wonder if you also by the long-suffering and humility implanted

[1] Zeph. i. 8. [2] 1 R. xvi. 4.

in you have brought about a serene and peaceful p. 156.
state of affairs[1] in place of the disturbance which had arisen? Wherefore we must also for everything praise and laud our God and Saviour Jesus Christ, our peace and tranquillity; who said to His disciples, "My peace I give unto you, my peace I leave unto you,"[2] and ordered them, to whomsoever they went, to say, "Peace to this house."[3] Pray therefore that we may be men worthy of this peace, in order that it may also abide with us and never leave us, now that we have once received it, as in fact it wishes, provided of course that we do not do anything contrary to it.

As to the religious Epimachus, because you the holy old man have, as you write, stretched the sinews of your mind and had recourse to the harshness of the strict execution of the canons owing to the admonitions that we gave,[4] ought we also to extend this matter further with them, and ourselves also to scratch (?) in a more violent manner that which has once been done, even though in an inconsiderate manner, and make it come to an ulcer and end by being incurable? By no means. But on the contrary, we ought to devise some remedy and carry it out, by some kind of healing friction and humane refreshment. It does not seem that we are running counter to the intention of the canons in allowing him to conduct the prayers only and so forth, but not to offer the sacred sacrifice.

[1] κατάστασις. [2] John xiv. 27. [3] Lu. x. 5. [4] i. 49.

Accordingly let him have both the title and the privileges of a presbyter, on account of his long continuance in the monastic life, and on account of the fact that he thereby as far as possible purified his previous life, and on account of the man's attested
p. 157. devoutness, and because neither did he himself seek to be raised to this position, but was raised against his will and submitted to the decision and nomination of others. In fact even on the former occasion I did not write to you as a lawgiver, but rather as performing a service. And I did not do this of my own accord, but because some great "necessity is laid upon me," as the Apostle says, and because "woe is unto me if I do not" serve necessity and so "preach the gospel."[1] Indeed, although the burden is heavy, yet still "I am entrusted with a stewardship,"[2] and, bowed down though I am, I must execute this with all fear and trembling. Still it would have been unjust that, because you "fear everything through devoutness," as it is written,[3] while I submit to the necessity of the laws, the man who came to ordination against his will as we have said should be injured and not receive refreshment. Whence under compulsion and as a consequence we have, as is possible, been brought to these second thoughts, seeing that we too are bowed down by the weight of many sins, and stand in need, if any man else besides, of the clemency of God. But may you, sacred man, be

[1] 1 Co. ix. 16. [2] *Ibid.*, 17. [3] Pr. xxviii. 14.

preserved for us in health and youthful vigour, being more powerfully strengthened with spiritual sinews, and correcting our paralysis, and putting forth wings and being renewed like the eagles,[1] and singing with the prophet David and saying, "And I will go in unto the altar of God, unto God that reneweth my youth!"[2]: and there offering prayers on our P. 158.
behalf.

As to the holy communion or oblation which is being sent to Alypius the poor child (so you often termed him in your letter) I have this much to say: that, if you had previously told his father also the very thing which you have often said, I mean that he ought not to be in doubt as to the existing state of things[3] in the holy churches in Alexandria and in Egypt, since it is now (to speak with God's permission) free from association and communion with heretics, you would perhaps now have had the courage to say that the revered and sacred communion or oblation must not be sent to him. But, since the thing has been thus begun and has become known to the adversaries, what necessity is there for us to do further harm, and go on to ruin the boy who is about as your sanctity says to yield to his grandfather? Let the child therefore be refreshed with the usual refreshment from you on account of his believing father, and not be neglected on account of his unbelieving grandfather. For it is written, "The thoughts of the righteous are judgments."[4] And henceforth for

[1] Ps. cii. 5. [2] *Id.*, xlii. 4. [3] κατάστασις. [4] Pr. xii. 5.

the future let us not turn aside to similar things, nor give occasion to those who seek occasion, nor in order to content one person disturb the whole church. Know well that I was loth to write that the believing Mitra ought to have sent his son to communicate with the
p. 159. church which by God's grace is clean and pure, the church which now looks to our banished self, and does not acquiesce in any cunning fraud. For, even though it had been right to send the often mentioned holy communion to the boy, how can it be anything but unreasonable that this boy should live with enemies, who reveal without shame even that which is thought to be ineffable?

And after other things. As to those who like the magnificent Anastasius are zealous for piety, and all who are settled in the land of the Philistines, who is there who is so wrathful and alien to the divine laws as to say that the communion or oblation ought not to be given them when they ask, to any extent that they wish and without stint? Our whole argument with you related to those who are residing in Alexandria and show doubts that are superfluous and intolerable because they inflicted injury on many. Do not therefore omit to give at the due time and to those who require it the indestructible grace, which as it is written was given for nothing,[1] and is being asked for for nothing. You know, even if we do not write it, how great punishment[2] and reproof from God is caused by

[1] Mt. x. 8. [2] ζημία.

neglect to give readily and without any hesitation. *The end.*

p. 160.

51. *Of the same to Philip the presbyter.* (*From those after banishment, from the 2nd book the 40th letter.*) **519-38.**

I have read the words written by your religiousness, not without sorrow, but with sympathy: not like a stranger but like a brother: not as one who is above law, but as one who is subject to law. Wherefore I am writing to you that you may rejoice, not that you may be distressed: that you may know yourself, not that you may despair. Do not think that what you have written needs a refutation of the same length. You perhaps made your letter so long from a desire to incline the reader to pity and draw attention to your purpose: but I listen to the sacred writings rather than to you: and in submission to the precise declaration of the Spirit I quote to you the ordinance of Koheleth which ordains that "there is a time for everything," and with the other things says this also, "A time to p. 161.
weep and a time to laugh, a time to mourn and a time to dance."[1] At the proper time, as you say, you confessed the sins of your youth to the common and holy fathers. But to me you made the confession at an improper time and after the fitting season; for I acquiesce in your written statement in order that you

[1] Ec. iii. 1, 4.

may know that, as the sacred text somewhere says, it is right to obey God under all circumstances.[1] But perhaps you will say that even now you have not missed the proper time, seeing that the canons admit the confession of great sins even after ordination, and exclude those who confess them from the sacred ministry, and allow them to share only the privileges and the name of the priesthood.[2] Know that I too am not unaware of this statute. But what can the effect upon me be when the Apostle cries, "The covenant which was before confirmed by God the law which was afterwards does not annul?"[3] I describe as the covenant of God the testimony given by our common teacher and father John, the great man of God, when he pre-
p. 162. sented you for ordination, and I heartily confirm it. It seems to me therefore great presumption for me to annul the testimony of a father of this character and such as he, or to add anything to this and give orders that go beyond it. For we all know that that man was not a doer of his own will, nor presumptuous in actions, but one who, if any other man besides, makes the blessing his own which is promised to those who "fear everything through devoutness."[4] Wherefore also I assuredly know that after the confession which you made of your sins, unless he had received confirmation by inspiration from above, he would not have advanced you to this rank. Whenever therefore any of the lapses that you committed in youth troubles your memory, recall

[1] Ac. v. 29 (?). [2] Mansi ii. 542. [3] Ga. iii. 17. [4] Pr. xxviii. 14.

your thoughts to him who gave you the testimony and forget yourself, and be "turned into another man,"[1] and boldly perform the duties proper to the sacred ministry: and do not show yourself excessive in devoutness and trust yourself to the pronouncements of the thoughts, lest you hear the sacred scripture reproving you and saying, "Be not righteous overmuch, neither make thyself over wise lest thou be astonied."[2] Whereas you are here, there, and everywhere representing p. 163.
second marriage as a thing that is less serious than the greatest sins and yet is excluded from priestly functions, know that such a conception falls outside the range of spiritual interpretation. A second marriage was granted by way of indulgence, as a support of weakness: and he who has resorted to this of his own will and by deliberate judgment has enrolled himself among those that are weak and have been granted an indulgence and are in the second order, and are not raised to the first sacred rank. It is therefore manifest presumption, and contempt of the sacred laws, for a man to enrol himself among those that are weak and objects of indulgence, and to do this with the law's aid and openly, and then strive to rise to the first sacred rank, which is composed of those who are sound. But a man who has sinned in the times of his youth has not fallen under sin because he judged it lawful to sin, but has committed an involuntary lapse, insomuch that he may be purified by penitence. I do not say this in

[1] 1 R. x. 6. [2] Ec. vii. 17.

order to show a second marriage to be a sin (far be it!); it is rather a support for weakness, that does not place those who are married outside the company of those who are saved, but assigns them a low rank.
p. 164. Incline your ear therefore to the divine law, and when it bids you perform priestly functions say the words that are written, "Speak, Lord, for thy bondsman heareth."[1] However, if for the present you shrink from offering[2] the perfect sacrifice, I will allow you to abstain for a time, but not to go so far as to bind yourself under such an inhibition. But in all other functions you shall not be restrained in any way whatever. *The end.*

520-25. 52. *Of the same to John and John the presbyters and the rest. (From those after banishment, from the 2nd book the 42nd letter.)*

I sent an answer at once to the earlier letter which reached me from your sanctity: and, because no ship was at hand, the letter was delayed several days: but I expect that you have by this time received it. As to the epistle that has just been sent, about the slave who was sold by the Jews and the question regarding him, I have nothing to write. For a letter was written by me about a similar matter to a certain Theodore the God-loving bishop of Olba (this is a city in Isauria),[3] and I have thought well to give an *ison* or

1 1 R. iii. 9. 2 ἀναφορά. 3 ix. 2.

copy of it at the end of this letter, so that from it you p. 165.
may know what our own conclusion was.

As to clergymen who come from outside, who hold the correct faith but are not united in communion with us, the answer is plain : *i.e.*, that we must not admit these men to the exercise of the ministry : but in all other respects, in order to promote sound and correct opinions, must hold intercourse with them as with our own people and extend goodwill towards them. If we do not do this, we shall, unknown to ourselves, be circumscribing, so to speak, the right ways of the Lord. But, if any man, being a clergyman, wishes to hold entirely aloof from communion with those to whom he is subject, let him go to the God-loving archbishop of the city of the Alexandrines or to the banished bishops, and the privileges of communion will be properly conceded to him by them. For your love of God it is a sufficient answer to these men to say that without the bishops you can do nothing, and this does not lie in your authority. By this plan you will be preserved from irregularity, and they from finding any occasion of stumbling or of offence.

As to those in Isauria and in First Cilicia, an epistle that has just been sent to us is very gloomy : and, not to say anything harsh, it accuses those of First Cilicia of remissness, and it announces a grievous
persecution and expulsion of the orthodox in Isauria, p. 166.
as well of the devout monks, as of the clergymen and of those who are among the believing people, not to speak of what has happened in consequence, that

all have abandoned communion with Stephen the disturber, the present prelate, and are not unaware of his treachery and falseness and the evil habits ingrained in him. The wretched man has even presumed to send some of the clergymen who have been corrupted by him here also to the saintly Isaurian bishops in banishment, as if summoning them to him, and heaping vanities upon vanities, as is written,[1] and "beating the air" in vain, as the Apostle says.[2] However these impious men do not cease from making confusion, and from audaciously attempting to no purpose even things that are impossible, and from polluting the water for drinking with their feet, in order to give those who are not cautious turbid pollution to drink according to the prophetic saying.[3] Isidore the illustrious tribune has started in peace for Pelusium, after promising the devout presbyter Thomas to do all things in accordance with God's pleasure. He had also after the conversation held here written to the devout presbyter Epimachus to tell his religiousness to go in the direction of Pelusium. In order therefore that you may not be ignorant of what has happened, this also has been added in this letter.

Console and comfort with loving disposition the God-loving Isidore bishop of the city of the men of
p. 167. Chalcis, who is troubled with a bodily infirmity, or rather who is being better proved in the furnace of trials; and reckon it all as a gift to me: though

[1] Ec. i. 3 (?). [2] 1 Co. ix. 26. [3] Eze. xxxiv. 18, 19.

I know that I am acting superfluously in this, since ready help and zealous attention in these matters are innate in you and belong to your character. For you must believe that I was much distressed when I learned that he had been again seized with the same kind of infirmity. *The end.*

53. *Of the same to the bishops from Syria in Alexandria. (From those after banishment, from the 2nd book the 64th letter.)* 519-20.

To the saintly God-loving brothers and fellow-ministers, the bishops who are under the apostolic see of the city of the Antiochenes, and are now settled in the great Christ-loving city of the Alexandrines, Cassian, Constantine, Antoninus, and the rest, Severus greeting in the Lord.

Though I am with your love of God in the spirit, I should have wished to be present in the flesh also, or, while absent in the body, to communicate with you more constantly through this remaining source of comfort, I mean by means of letters, concerning the hope laid down beforehand for those who have believed in Christ. But, since, when men are living p. 168.
without fear, every time is convenient to them for sending letters, but, when they are under constraint or imprisoned, it does not lie in their power to do this, even against their will they check and silence the ardour of affection: but when need demands they then cut the fetters of constraint, and do not submit

to the ropes that fall to them among the strong, to speak in the words of the Psalmist,[1] but move their tongue, and serve the divine law. For this reason Paul used to say that he "endured evil things as an evildoer even to bonds for the Gospel's sake," but that "the word of God was not bound."[2] Therefore I also the mean one look to that pattern and say, and that very justly, "Though I flee for Christ's sake, yet His word has not fled; for it is present in every place where the law of the Spirit wishes to carry it." Therefore I salute you, and embrace you, the sharers of my flight, whose feet are beautiful, who do not preach,[3] but by accepting persecution as the law requires walk aright and follow Him who said, "When they persecute you in this city flee to another";[4] or perhaps it is better to say that by the very fact of being persecuted you loudly proclaim the gospel, and by the fact of being silent speak. Therefore, since you have been brought to such honour, Christ who is persecuted with you is present with you also, and He is a chief and leader for you in purpose and in
p. 169. commands. Those who were removed to the land of Babylon, and endeavoured there also to live in accordance with the law, and were bereft of the sacred fane and the service, and did not even sing a song, because it was not lawful to do any of these things outside the tabernacle or outside the sanctuary,[5]

[1] Ps. xv. 6. [2] 2 Ti. ii. 9. [3] Is. lii. 7. [4] Mt. x. 23.
[5] Ps. cxxxvi. 2–4.

but still set themselves to live in accordance with their fathers' customs and to pronounce right judgments had the Holy Spirit dwelling in them, insomuch that the divine Daniel being most divinely inspired from that source convicted those wicked elders, and those three boys not only performed a miracle by exulting in the furnace, the burning effect of the fire having been assuaged, but also sang a prophetic hymn of praise. Who is there therefore who will not say with greater justice that the Holy Spirit is dwelling among you, even when you are settled by the evangelic throne of the holy Mark, and are dwelling in a very loyal city, one whose special possession and high honour in addition to its other excellences is correctness and distinction in the faith, and as a chief and leader and counsellor and good teacher of everything that ought to be done and counselled you have the saintly Timothy the archbishop of this city, a man who not only fills the place of my meanness, but is even able to shelter me owing to his high position? Hence also the case of the religious Paul, formerly bishop of Olba in Isauria, has been very well treated by you and brought to a very proper conclusion: and this resolution that you have adopted is not at variance p. 170.
with the sacred ecclesiastical ordinances. For a time of persecution more particularly invites us to be more than ordinarily mild, and to gather together the scattered limbs of the church, and to block the exits of unreasonable schisms. Secondly, if one understand the *diataxeis* or canonical commands also not accord-

ing to the letter after the manner of a Jew, but according to the spirit and intention of the church law, one will find that they desire that a bishop who has been unanimously deprived by the synod in the province[1] shall in those cases only be denied restoration in another synod when the synod that has pronounced his deposition remains in the same mind. For the eighty-fourth canon says as follows: "If anyone has been excommunicated by his own bishop, he shall not be received by others unless he has first been received by his bishop himself, or a synod has been held and he has presented himself, and made a defence, and has persuaded the synod and received another verdict. And the same rule applies also to laymen and presbyters and deacons and all that are included in the canon."[2] The ninetieth canon also says as follows: "If any presbyter or deacon shall be deprived by his bishop, or a bishop also by a synod, and shall dare to trouble the king's ears,
p. 171. and, when he should betake himself to a greater synod of bishops and offer the pleas which he thinks he has to a larger number of bishops, and accept examination and judgment from them, shall treat these with contempt and trouble the king, these men shall not receive any forgiveness, nor shall an opportunity of defence be allowed them, nor shall they expect any hope of future restoration."[3] It is therefore manifest from this too that it is possible for a man who has

[1] ἐπαρχία. [2] Mansi ii. 1312. [3] *Ibid.*, 1313.

been deprived by a smaller synod to be received in a greater one if the charges and complaints against him are examined and investigated afresh. It is in a sense similar to this that the eighty-second canon also is to be understood, which says: [Here follows the citation given at p. 124]. For the substance of these three canons is this: that, when a man has been deprived by a small synod, it is possible for him to discuss the causes of his deprivation before a greater synod and obtain restoration, if the great synod decide to absolve this man. But, if he shall dare after his deprivation to perform any priestly function, even access to a greater synod shall be refused him, if those who have once effected his deprivation continue to maintain the same judgment of deprivation. For the whole purpose of the canons is directed to this; that the verdicts[1] of those who p. 172.
have duly decided shall not be annulled, so long as they continue to maintain their verdict[2] which they have pronounced. But, if these men (I mean those who deprived the man) with the same unanimity recede from the unfavourable verdict,[2] and betake themselves to another which absolves him, how can anyone doubt that the forgiveness is certainly warranted by law, especially if another synod greater than it also confirms this? If therefore the saintly bishops in Isauria who effected the deprivation of Paul and his companions continued to maintain the same ver-

[1] ἀποφάσεις.

[2] ἀπόφασις.

dict[1] of deprivation, it is absolutely necessary that the severity of these canons shall prevail, and that the punishment which was inflicted upon them shall be in no point annulled by the authority of a greater synod. But, if they also all alike consented to absolve those who were condemned, and Solon also of saintly memory, the bishop of their metropolis, acquiesced in this decision, we for our part will not show ourselves harsh searchers of the canons, which in no way prevented those who have deprived a man from coming to a more lenient state of mind, but laid down a law and issued a command regarding another synod, saying that it has no right to lay additional commands, to speak in the words of the Apostle, upon the bishops who effected the
p. 173. deprivation, and tyrannically to annul the judgment given by these. We find that the holy fathers for the benefit of the churches often receded and granted an indulgence even after sentence of deprivation had been passed by a catholic and œcumenical synod, for the sake of the general benefit and peace of the churches themselves. For instance in the holy synod at Ephesus Helladius of Tarsus and Eutherius of Tyana, and Dorotheus and Himerius were deprived together with Nestorius, on the ground that they were infected with opinions akin in impiety, and were afflicted with the same madness as he to a greater extent than the others. And yet afterwards, when the bishops of

[1] ἀπόφασις.

the East had abandoned the unreasonable schism and submitted to the resolutions of the holy œcumenical synod which assembled in the city of the Ephesians, upon Paul bishop of the city of the Emesenes coming to the city of the Alexandrines and on their behalf asking Cyril the chief champion of orthodoxy, a man who in apostolic contests endured dangers even to death, that they might remain in their sees in the p. 174
position which they actually held he waived the deprivation of the said wicked men, insisting only on this point which was more particularly necessary, I mean that the deprivation of Nestorius should be confirmed by all of them together and in writing, and that they should confess that the holy Virgin is the God-bearer and such conditions as follow upon these. This he stated in the letter to Eusebius the presbyter, in which he wrote as follows: "I have read the letter from your devoutness: and I have found you to be distressed by the supposition that the peace of the churches has been completed upon an unreasonable basis; but I imagined that it was by love that your gentleness was moved. However it is probable that you have no accurate knowledge of the points settled. For certain persons are, I learn, circulating letters purporting to have been written to me by the devout and religious bishop John. But it is probable that either they are forgeries or they contain additions made to please those who hold the opinions of Nestorius. For, in accordance with the resolution of the holy synod in the metropolis of the Ephesians, I did

not give him communion until he had anathematized in writing the doctrines of Nestorius, and confessed that he held him to be under deprivation, and assented to the ordination of the devout God-loving bishop Maximian. But when the religious Paul bishop of the city of the Emesenes exerted himself vigorously on
p. 175. behalf of those who had been deprived, Helladius I mean and Eutherius and Dorotheus and Himerius, and begged that, when the peace of the churches was established, their case[1] also might receive a *typos* or determination, I used these words: 'I do not take any account of those who have been deprived: but they must remain in the position in which they in fact are now.' But the insult which they levelled against me I have forgiven. For it was not indeed fitting that for this reason and no other the churches should fall into a state of schism and division, when the more necessary point was brought to a conclusion, I mean the requirement that the doctrines of Nestorius should be anathematized and his deprivation acknowledged by those who would not do this before, and they also confessed in writing that the holy Virgin is the God-bearer."[2] This generous forgiveness he bestowed, for the sake of the peace and union of the holy churches, upon men who, as the succeeding time showed, were incurable. And yet he endured for the sake of an object that was better and of higher advantage, I mean for the sake of the unification and binding together of

[1] ὑπόθεσις.

[2] Ep. 54.

the more important limbs. For in the same letter he added these words also: "For, even though Helladius in Tarsus and certain others do not think rightly, this p. 176.
has nothing to do with those who wish to think what is right. For let two or three go if they wish, so long as the churches everywhere hold one and the same faith." How then are we for our part not bound to regard the mind of those who fed and governed the churches of God with such understanding, and to conclude that the course sanctioned by you in the instance of the religious Paul must also be followed in that of the devout bishop Elpidius, particularly since Paul as I have learned during the time of his deprivation presumed so far as to attempt the performance of high-priestly acts or services, but Elpidius, they say, did nothing whatever of the kind. I forbear to mention also the celebrated case[1] of the holy John who was bishop of Constantinople. Since you read church histories, you know that he incurred deprivation; but, because of his reputation for right teaching and in order that those in the royal city who were in separation on account of the mention of his name might be reconciled to the body of the church, the holy Cyril waived the point, being apostolically minded in this matter also, and not seeking his own but that which belongs to Christ Jesus,[2] and setting the benefit of ecclesiastical p. 177.
union and reconciliation against all subtle words and strict procedure, and that though in letters he often

[1] ὑπόθεσις.

[2] Ph. ii. 21.

contended for canonical strictness. Therefore I bestow all praise upon the whole of your God-loving synod, seeing it both examined the demands of strictness, and at the same also considered the suggestions of a benevolent mind. In fact both those who desired strict procedure did so because they took account of preserving an appearance worthy of confidence and suited to the church, and equally also those who inclined to mild measures were not of this opinion because they had anything else at heart than to bring about a bond of peace and to gather together those who were dispersed. However in such cases as these that plan must be followed which gathers together the limbs of the church and has clemency as a superfluous advocate, and the example of the fathers who were thus minded in similar cases, and thus provided for what lay before them. Do not therefore think to yourselves that you did anything unreasonable in discussing this matter with one another (it is not right or proper for us to say that you were divided). Did not this happen among the apostles also? The book of the Acts relates that "certain men had come down from Judæa and were teaching the brethren, saying, 'Unless ye are circum-
p. 178. cised after the custom of Moses, ye cannot have life': and, as Paul and Barnabas had no small dissension and dispute with them,"[1] the disputation passed to other churches also, until Peter the chief of the apostles and James, who was termed brother of our Lord, but had

[1] Ac. xv. 1, 2.

received the first episcopal office in Jerusalem, were inspired from above, and brought forward the prophetic words, and so put an end to the dispute that had been raised: and they extended their resolution to the other churches also, so that all members of all of them might say the same and think the same. I forbear to say that there was a quarrel not only about doctrines but also about a person between Paul and Barnabas, since the one said that they ought to take John who was called Mark with them on their preaching, while the other said not. These things are written as a pattern for us, in order that we may not fear and be caused to fall. It is not possible that being men we should not be angered: but, if we are angered, we must turn from our anger. Therefore in the case of Paul and Elpidius the devout bishops also let the suggestions of a benevolent mind and the course of forgiveness prevail, and let them share in the privileges and title of bishops, but not thrust themselves into their cities, if the time p. 179.
invite to this, seeing that other God-loving bishops have once been lawfully designated to their sees, nor have any share in the rights belonging to that parish: a principle which, as I have been told, they have in fact with great propriety as well as with much justice acknowledged to you in writing. For they also shall not lack any kind of consolation which, while consistent with the canons, will not cause any useless annoyance or injury to anyone, if it take place here. For indeed "our life is swifter than a runner,"[1] as it is written:

[1] Job ix. 25.

and "what the day that is coming will bring forth" we know not at all.[1] I have written this epistle while suffering the affliction of a fugitive and unable to set foot in . . . . as it is written. . . . . and, as . . . . says, no book and no . . . . surrounds me. But . . . . remembering the sacred . . . . and . . . . in [my] memory the laws and customs also that were practised from of old in the holy churches. Wherefore also I have both received and duly praised the resolutions canonically adopted by you and inserted in an epistle concerning those in the Christ-loving city of the Antiochenes who wish to come to repentance. For they were lawful and proper,
p. 180. and such as, while not falling outside the limits of what is lawful, bore the marks of a loving disposition and of clemency. If anything else also of this kind should happen, ...

519-38. 54. . . . .

in truth that the mouth should be silent which never grows weary and seems as if it had been set apart for prayers, the mouth which in very deed says "I will bless the Lord at all times,"[2] and at all times circulates His praises. You did well and conferred a great service upon us by relating in the course of your letter how you celebrated the memories of the holy fathers, and which of you have departed to God, one among whom is the religious presbyter Patrick. We are much profited

[1] Pr. xxvii. 1.

[2] Ps. xxxiii. 1.

when we learn the names of these in order that we may remember them in our prayers, and as far as possible, cast from us the weariness that dominates us, and prepare ourselves for the final departure from this world.

As to the events that have happened in the East, and the way in which the believers in Antioch have girded themselves for a second and third contest, as if they had never been tried by any tribulation, it is superfluous for us to write to you, since these are things which you learn also from report. Only we ask you to keep those who are thus combating in more earnest remembrance, and to ask that endurance may be granted them all by God. In trials which are so unendurable it is in fact impossible to be steadfast without help from that source. Wherefore Jeremiah p. 181.
also said to God over all, "Lord, the endurance of Israel! Thou savest in the time of evils."[1] But I beg your holinesses to grant a place among those who are remembered by you over the rational sacrifice and have already gone to God to Eustochius of God-loving memory, deacon of the holy church in Alexandria, who has now put off his life in much zeal for the orthodox faith, with all accuracy and in knowledge as the divine Apostle says,[2] so that he often longed for the bodily sight of your love of God also. Of him the religious presbyter Philip also made trial to a moderate extent. *The end.*

[1] Jer. xiv. 8.

[2] 1 Co. i. 5; Ph. i. 9 (?).

525-31. 55. *Of the same to Theodore presbyter and archimandrite of the monastery of father Romanus among the saints.* (*From those after banishment, from the 3rd book the 32nd letter.*)

Even I, though I am in hiding and live in different places at different times on account of the present stress, was not unaware of your religiousness' praiseworthy life. Wherefore also I thought the expressions
p. 182. of John the Evangelist and Apostle fitted to be addressed to you by me, which he composed when writing an epistle to someone and speaking thus: "I rejoiced greatly when brethren came and testified to the truth that is in thee, how that thou walkest in the truth."[1] Continue therefore to show the same energy, and press forwards, and enlarge the rational flock of those who practise with you the ascetic life of solitariness, and let them henceforth have a 'measure of wheat' of the doctrines of philosophy with understanding, as the gospel text advises; which also promises a blessing to him who does this carefully and with diligence, saying, "Blessed is the bondservant whom his lord shall come and find so doing. Of a truth I say unto you that he will set him over all that he hath."[2] The question also that you have now been pleased to ask of the religious presbyter Thomas by your letter was in truth in consonance with your

[1] 3 J. 3.

[2] Lu. xii. 42–44.

understanding. For he sent me the letter that you wrote, and, when it came to my knowledge, I praised it. And, owing to the urgency of the matter, I considered it right to treat all other things as secondary, and send you this mean letter: in which it is pointed out that all of you who hold to communion with us must not recognise any distinction between those who are banished from the East, and made illustrious by the combat of confessorship, and the saintly bishops in Egypt, and that you must reckon that to be one church which is compacted together in the orthodox faith, and confession and communion, and is most pure and free from the no-association with the heretics; p. 183.
and that you must also have no vain hesitation about ordinations: but that both your religiousness and the other religious archimandrites of the holy cloisters that have been banished from Palestine[1] on account of the word of truth must after probation present your own brethren to the God-loving bishops in Egypt, in order that they may ordain presbyters and deacons for you, and satisfy the requirements of your need. How is it anything but an unreasonable state of affairs and one fraught with matter for every kind of accusation that, while the bishops who have been banished from other countries and bear upon them marks for Christ's sake flee to the great orthodox apostolic church in Alexandria as to a mother, certain men out of a childish mind should create a distinction that does not

[1] This was therefore written during the exile of the monks (Zach Rh. viii. 5).

exist between those who are thus united and make up the compact union of the limbs of the one body, and through the very facts themselves proclaim the immobility and steadfastness of the holy persecuted churches in the East and those in Egypt, which are already preparing to suffer the same things, and showing the immoveable nature of their piety? I think that the events which happened a short time ago in Alexandria have reached your ears also, events capable of showing even to those who are very foolish
p. 184. the steadfastness and fixedness of the saintly archbishop Timothy, and of the God-loving bishops under him, and of the churches in their cities: so that one may fitly utter the celebrated expressions of Isaiah the prophet, "Tabernacles that shall not shake; nor shall the pegs of her tabernacle be moved for ever, and her cords shall not be broken asunder."[1] Therefore for a man to try to separate by vain thoughts things that are so admirably united, and to divide things that are so indivisible through the inspiration of grace from above is a thing fraught with matter for every kind of evil-speaking and fault-finding. This we warn both your love of God and all who communicate with us to shun, and to cast such stones of stumbling out of the Lord's ways as it is written,[2] and, as we said before, to reckon the ordination of the saintly bishops of the East and that of those of Egypt to be one, and not recognise any distinction between these. If you wish to read

[1] Is. xxxiii. 20.

[2] *Id.*, lvii. 14 (?).

this letter to any other persons also, in order to show what our opinion is, neither do we forbid this. How can it not be right that we should also proclaim openly in words the things that we in actual practice think and do? *The end.*

p. 185.

56. *Of the same to Proclus the bishop.* (*From those after expulsion, from the 3rd book the 36th letter*). **519-38.**

The words that I wrote to the two of you in common[1] were enough to show[2] your love of God my opinion, since you thought me at all competent to give advice. For my part, since "I have boldness of speech towards you," as Paul says to the Corinthians,[3] I thought that, inasmuch as you have been brought up from the earliest times in works of piety, and have stood with us from the beginning, and borne the assaults of many waves, that you are competent to give advice and direction to others also in what is right. However choice is an evil thing, evil indeed, and may involve even wise men in ruin in adverse times, for, "they were confounded and staggered like a drunken man, and all their wisdom was swallowed up,"[4] says he that sings figuratively and instructively. Wherefore I myself also recognise our nature's feebleness, and, inasmuch as I am subject to the same weaknesses, I grant you forgiveness for having

[1] v. 13.

[2] Whether the following to p. 170, l. 4, belongs to this letter is doubtful: see vol. i., Intr.

[3] 2 Co. vii. 4.

[4] Ps. cvi. 27.

shown a common weakness and being in need of encouragement. Perhaps also some thoughts are springing up in your heart, which put such ideas as these into you and say, "This man, because he has nothing to do with the affairs of the world, and is not assailed
p. 186. by trouble of this sort, and does not know what kind of thing is the tie of nature that arises from the marriage connexion and the birth of children, will give you impassioned advice from beyond the boundaries, and will speak as from some exalted height with those that creep upon the earth." Therefore in answer to these things also we must use introductory words and say what is the truth. Paul the wise man and chosen vessel, who had Christ so firmly established in him that in giving ecclesiastical commandments he would sometimes appeal to the laws of Christ, and draw his admonitions from them, and at another put forward his own thoughts in place of a law and say, "I have no commandment of the Lord; but I give counsel; inasmuch as I have obtained mercy of the Lord to be a believer,"[1] when appointing bishops, did not take men from the training-school of the solitary life and set them over the churches, nor men of philosophic habits, free from wives, and without children, but he said, "The bishop ought to be the husband of one wife," and, "one that ruleth his house well and hath his children in subjection with all gravity";[2] and he was not assured as regards these ties of nature, the ties of

[1] 1 Co. vii. 25.

[2] 1 Ti. iii. 2, 4.

children I mean and of a wife, that they would corrupt the character of a shepherd in times of stress. But, as to what the character of a shepherd is, hear the shepherd Himself crying and saying, "The good shepherd layeth down his life for his sheep."[1] If therefore we have been called by Him to so great a height of p. 187.
spiritual authority, it is absolutely necessary that we should rise to the same height, and that we should "mind high things" and "seek the things which are above, where Christ is, sitting on the right hand of God": so that, when He "is revealed," then we "also may be revealed with Him in glory,"[2] and share with Him in splendour. But, that you may not think to yourself that you alone among bishops have had a wife and children, and are required to "resist sin even to blood," as it is written,[3] and to distinguish yourself in combats on behalf of piety, the words of the apostolic legislation that have just been quoted, words that have a general application to every bishop, would in themselves have been sufficient answer to such a fancy: but I will quote to you from actual experience also an example worthy of consideration, which shows that in times of martyrdom the women also who were joined in marriage to those who held the rank of the episcopate contested and strove in the same contests. Here it is. Dionysius, who was bishop of the great Christ-loving city of the Alexandrines, in an epistle to Flavian[4] bishop of

[1] John x. 11.

[2] Col. iii. 1, 2, 4.

[3] He. xii. 4

[4] Fabius is meant.

Antioch, in which he describes the combats of those who were martyred in the neighbourhood of Alexander's city in the days of Decius, after describing the other events introduces this statement also :[1] . . .

. . . .

p. 188. in sin, and utterly refuses to turn her eyes upwards while there is time. For for you, who bear with patience that which has happened in this matter also, a worthy reward will surely be reserved, although you did not treat her case with circumspection at the beginning. But, if you both exert yourself and bring her back from the error in which she is involved to repentance and recognition of the truth, then you will in truth be doubly a father to her, insomuch as to be able to say, "Behold! I and the children whom God has given me."[2] For you must do all these things to the best of your power, in order that you may not have your conscience accusing you, as if you ought to have done something and had neglected it. You know well from the sacred writings what Eli suffered, because, though he spoke reprovingly to his sons and chid their folly in the unhallowed deeds which they committed, yet he did not deal with them as a ruler. But the Lord will, I know well, grant your sanctity understanding, so that with fatherly admonitions you may mingle such censures as are likely to produce conversion and are suited to a ruler, and that you may take the sheep upon your shoulders, and present it to the chief shepherd Christ,

[1] Eus. H.E. vi. 41. [2] Is. viii. 18.

and reckon it among those that are saved. For indeed He alone is able by His almighty power and His grace to make things possible that with men are impossible. *The end.*

p. 189.

57. *Of the same to Didymus the bishop.* (*From those after banishment, from the 3rd book the 50th letter.*) **519-25.**

The news of the attack of the barbarians [1] and of the captivity that has fallen upon those who live in your neighbourhood, and the siege and war that have been hanging over your city have caused intolerable grief and sorrow to all who hear of it, but especially to us. Our anxiety on other grounds and general sorrow was further increased by thinking of your religiousness, who have had to endure such an unexpected attack at the very beginning of your episcopate : since men who have been admitted to feed rational souls reckon common and public [2] calamities as their own. Wherefore David also the great among prophets and kings, when he saw his subjects being destroyed in the death-dealing plague by the divine wrath, being unable to endure the sight, begged that he might suffer instead of those under his rule, saying to the Lord, "It is I who have sinned, and I the shepherd have done wickedly : and these the sheep what have they done? Let thine hand be upon me, and upon my father's house." [3]

[1] Probably the incursion of Al Mundhir (Zach. Rh. viii. 5).

[2] δημόσια.

[3] 2 R. xxiv. 17.

And by so saying he changed the wrath to mercy, and stayed the plague. Therefore you also must know that such events are fraught with no small hardship: but, when men consider things in the right spirit, and
p. 190. accept the chastisement as a help, they bring them great profit, and lead them into close relationship with God. Therefore we also, looking at what has happened, believe that it is by divine providence that you have been raised to a sacred headship of this kind, in order that you may show yourself a man capable of comforting the flock that has been entrusted to you. As to the question that you ask about presbyters who have grown very old, I mean whether their customary share in the distribution of presents ought to be cut off from them, on the ground that they cannot perform the sacred ministry, and others introduced in their place who ought to be supported, and receive the
p. 191. portion cut off from these, know that such a thing is not legal, nor otherwise holy. If men who perform bodily services as soldiers for kings on earth, when they reach old age, receive higher stipends, inasmuch as they have previously toiled and laboured in wars, how is it anything but abominable that men who have served in the sacred military service should not only not receive higher honour in their old age, but even be deprived of the customary emoluments? David's soldiers also once thought something like this, when they went down with him to fight against the barbarians who had come against them, and mightily overcame them, and stripped them of all the booty

that had been carried off by them from the wars[1] with Israel. For, when they returned from the war and their minds were somewhat uplifted on account of their victory, they claimed that they alone should take all the things that they had captured from the barbarians, and not give an equal portion to those who stayed in the camp and guarded their baggage, on p. 192.
the ground that they had not taken part with them in the fight in exactly the same fashion. And upon this the just David was indignant, saying that those also who remained to guard the baggage ought to get a portion equal to that of those who formed part of the array in war. Moreover also he repressed their greed and said to them in rebuke, "And who will hearken to these words of yours? For they are not inferior to you. But, as his portion is that went down to the war, so shall his portion be that stayed by the baggage. They shall part alike."[2] Knowing therefore from the divine writings that these things are laid down as law, give greater gratification, if possible, to those who have grown old, both in stipends and in honour. For honour is the due of elders, and the enjoyment of the good things that come after war. The great governor Moses also wrote in Numbers that he said to Hobab his wife's brother, who was journeying with Israel in the way in the wilderness, "Leave us not, forasmuch as thou wast with us in the wilderness. And thou shalt be an

[1] The translator therefore read πολέμων for πόλεων.

[2] 1 R. xxx. 24.

elder among us. And it shall be, if thou go with us, we will do thee good out of all the good things which the Lord shall do unto us."[1] But I beg your love of God not to associate indiscriminately with those who unreasonably cut themselves off from our communion, men who magnify with lips only an orthodoxy that is inactive and runs no risk, while they take no part in the sufferings of the persecuted church which it has
p. 193. suffered for the sake of the sound word of faith and is still even now suffering, but justify themselves in vain. Lack of discrimination towards them confirms them yet more in the evil itself, and they think to themselves that we blame ourselves as if there had been something wanting in our conduct, and honour and praise them as men of strictness. We listen also to our Saviour in the Gospels crying, "He that is not with me is against me: and he that gathereth not with me scattereth."[2] Ignatius also the great bishop and martyr, who fed the church of the Antiochenes after Peter the captain of the apostles, and, because he was full of the Holy Spirit, was called "the God-clad," says in his letter to the men of Smyrna, "Shun divisions, as the beginning of evils."[3] Further also in another letter of his to those at Philadelphia he says thus: "If anyone follows a man who makes a schism, he does not inherit the kingdom of God."[4] Again in writing to the Ephesians he expresses the same thing in a more fearful form, saying, "He therefore that

[1] Nu. x. 31, 32. [2] Lu. xi. 23. [3] Sm. 8. [4] Phila. 3.

does not join in the assembly has already behaved proudly, and separated himself. For it is written, 'The proud God resisteth.'"[1] Irenæus also a man of ancient times, bishop of the city of Lyons (this is one of the cities of the men called Gauls), who was a hearer of Polycarp bishop of Smyrna and martyr, who p. 194.
was a disciple of John the Evangelist, wrote thus, in his fourth book against heresies, about the Lord who will judge every breathing thing, and as it is written the whole "world in righteousness"[2]: "But he will also judge those who create schisms, who are men void of the love of God, and seek that which is for their profit but not the union of the church, and for small and contemptible reasons cleave and divide the great and glorious body of Christ and, as far as in them lies, destroy it, men who speak peace and make war, who truly strain out the gnat, but swallow the camel. For it is impossible that any benefit can spring from them of the same kind as is the injury that springs from their schism."[3] To these things therefore direct your mind, and beware of the obstructive forces everywhere: especially of those that arise from thoughts on the right side, which lead astray from the "royal road"[4]: and, looking to heaven and making God your guide in all things, cry, "Direct my paths according to thy word"[5]; and you will surely go straight, and not fail to do what is right. *The end.*

[1] Eph. 5. [2] Ps. ix. 9. [3] Adv. Hær. IV. xxxiii. 7 (62).
[4] Nu. xx. 17. [5] Pr. iii. 6 (?).

p. 195.

519-25. 58. *Of the same to Didymus the bishop. (From those after banishment, from the 3rd book the 90th letter.)*

I have learned with accuracy the whole story of the devout deacon Sannus: and how before coming to the see where your love of God is priest he lived an indiscriminate or disordered life, and how you brought him back to devout habits, and how you laid down an injunction for him to keep. Now after examining the whole matter I have found that, because he appropriated to himself some small sum which formed part of the revenue, you were wroth and angry with him, and removed him from the charge with which he had been entrusted. Therefore I beg you to receive this man, and place him in the same rank, without any difference whatever. If by careful observance he observed all the other points on which reform was difficult, and gave up the long-standing practice of disorderly habits, which is like a necessity of nature, and was converted to a devout life, and took upon him the character proper to deacons, let us not upset everything on account of a sin in one single point: for it is impossible for everything to be reformed at once. This is the practice of teachers also, gently to bear with pupils once and twice and many times, when they are at fault and do not repeat without mistake, until they
p. 196. attain to perfection. Physicians also after the same fashion, when they warn patients to abstain from things

that are pleasant and harmful, are often defeated and grant them indulgences, allowing them to taste some of the things that they like: and they do not in every point insist upon strict observance of the irksome methods demanded by science, but they treat the patient in accordance with what is possible. This method of gradual treatment and cure was shown in a figurative manner by our Lord and God Jesus Christ also in the Gospels. When He might have healed one of the blind men who were brought to Him by word only, as He did in the case of that leper, saying in a manner befitting God, "I will be thou clean,"[1] and immediately upon the word completed the cure, He cured him with a certain delay and procrastination. For "He led him," he says, "out of the village. And, when He had spat on his eyes, He put His hands upon him and was asking him if he saw aught. And, his eyes having been opened, he said, 'I see the men walking like trees.' Then He put His hands again upon his eyes and his sight was restored and his eyes were opened, and he saw everything clearly."[2] Therefore He that is our God and the instructor of our souls by working this cure with a certain wise delay instructs us that the bishops in His holy churches, who are His representatives, ought to make use of gradual modes of treatment in order to bring those whose minds are blinded to the light, until their eyes are p. 197.
gradually opened and they see the rays of truth clearly.

[1] Mt. viii. 3. [2] Mk. viii. 23–25.

Accordingly do you also adopt this plan, both in this present affair and in others that happen after the same pattern. *The end.*

522-27. 59. *Of the same to Julian the presbyter and archimandrite of the monastery of the blessed Bassus. (From those during banishment, from the 5th book the 52nd letter.)*

Those who loyally follow the ascetic and solitary life grow rich in the spirit of understanding, and from it learn the paths of right action. Wherefore also the sacred text of Proverbs says, "The thoughts of an understanding man are ways of life":[1] and again "Let the heart of a man think just things, in order that his steps may be directed by the Lord."[2] Sharing in this instruction therefore and being guided by the divine Spirit, your religiousness also has not treated church order with contempt: but, when the holy monastery of the blessed Bassus, in which you have been appointed to be governor, was lacking in the needful provision for the ministry of priests and deacons, you properly
p. 198. resolved to inform me of this by a letter from you, and from me to obtain a solution of the doubt. Know therefore that in times of persecution anyone soever of the God-loving bishops who is of the same confession and the same communion with us in everything may properly supply the need of any among the orthodox who is in need. On this principle I have written to

[1] Pr. xv. 24

[2] *Id.*, xvi. 1.

the saintly Sergius bishop of Cyrrhus, and to the saintly Marion bishop of the fortress called Sura[1] to satisfy your need: and under the inspiration of the Holy Spirit to apply their sacred hand, and impart to those that are in need the gift that was given them from above, about which Jesus Himself the giver of the Spirit cries in the Gospels, "Freely ye have received freely give."[2] *The end.*

60. *Of the same to Photius and Andrew the presbyters and archimandrites of the holy cloisters in Caria. (From those after banishment, from the 7th book the 15th letter.)* **519-38.**

Since you loyally fulfil the active part of the ascetic and philosophic life, therefore you also gather the fruits of knowledge from your labours, which are sound faith and zeal on its behalf which raises itself to God, and devoutness and a spirit of understanding and of discretion. . . . .

. . . .

[You[3] also therefore, who through practice in asceticism are pure in your minds, in the same manner burn in the spirit, and carry the flame of zeal blazing in you: knowing as you do that all zeal is not praiseworthy, but that which is according to knowledge.

p. 199.

[1] v. 15.

[2] Mt. x. 8.

[3] The bracketed portion is supplied from another version: see text p. 199 note 1.

For you listen to Paul accusing the Jews and saying, "For I bear record of them that there is a zeal of God in them: but not according to knowledge":[1] and you have restrained the ardour of zeal with the cords of devoutness: for "blessed is the man that feareth all things on account of devoutness."[2] The case of the man who was received by you to communion and was converted from the heresy of the Nestorians and the Diphysites and the believers in two persons to the orthodox faith and said that he had received ordination to the diaconate you have thought fit to bring to the
p. 200. knowledge of my meanness, and learn whether you received this man lawfully and in accordance with the strictness of the canons or not. We say therefore that, in so far as you required him to anathematize on oath and in writing the heresy of the Nestorians and of the Diphysites, and renounce communion with them, the transaction was good and lawful: and he should not otherwise have shared in the reception of the divine mysteries, unless he had after this model done something to satisfy the mind. But neither should he have been presented for the ministry of the diaconate at all, nor on the other hand should he have proclaimed in writing the diaconal rank. For no canon or precept orders that those who have been converted from the heresy of the Nestorians shall receive ordination afresh. If they received ordination afresh, those also besides who were bap-

[1] Ro. x. 2. [2] Pr. xxviii. 14.

tized by the same heresy would always be baptized afresh. For, when men who have received ordination from particular heresies receive the laying on of hands afresh, those also who have been baptized by those very same heresies are baptized afresh : as the synod of the three hundred and eighteen holy fathers ordered in the case of the heresy of Paul of Samosata, and the heresies of those who are like them in impiety.[1] And no one has ever been shown to have perfected by a second baptism those who flee from] the Nestorian p. 201.
and Diphysite heresy, and have taken refuge in the church of the orthodox. Timothy also of saintly memory, archbishop of the city of the Alexandrines, who wrote in more severe terms from exile owing to the extreme ardour of the people, which would not consent even to cast a glance at those who derived ordination from the Diphysite error, which Proterius introduced there, after his return both communicated with Paul of God-loving memory, high-priest of the city of the Ephesians and head of the holy churches in Asia, in the Encyclical formula, upon his anathematizing with the bishops under him the Chalcedonian impiety : and also, after he had reached Alexandria, received those who came from the heresy of the Diphysites in the rank in which they were,[2] bishops I mean and presbyters and deacons, upon their anathematizing the heresy itself in writing, and accepting such a period of separation for peni-

[1] Mansi ii. 676. [2] *Cf.* v. 6.

tence only as he judged and determined to be good. In such cases in fact it is in the discretion
p. 202. of high-priests to shorten and to extend the spaces of time according to the consciousness of the penitents with regard to the sins committed by them. But he has not been shown to have done anything else whatever as to these men which impairs or disturbs the strictness of the canons in any point whatsoever; no second ordination, no second baptism, no chrism; as some from unreasonable fervour and inconsiderate zeal dared to do, at the beginning immediately after the synod at Chalcedon had been held, and became a cause of schisms and of divisions. For this reason also, after the holy Timothy of whom we are now speaking had thus received those who came from the error of Proterius and of the Diphysite heresy in accordance with the laws of the apostolic church, many men, fired as it were by some disorderly madness and self-willed ardour, separated from communion with him, while they did their best to inflame others also
p. 203. among those who were more than ordinarily weak, like those who said, "We have no part in David, neither inheritance in the son of Jesse,"[1] and divided Israel into two. Hence also they ascribed to them the name of the Novatians[2] who do not accept penitence for sins committed; and for a long time they disturbed the church, although they gradually melted away, and as the book of the Acts says "were scattered and

[1] 3 R. xii. 24 t.

[2] *Cf.* Zach. Rh. v. 4.

came to naught,"[1] like the rebellious band and seditious flock of Theudas and of Judas the Galilæan. These things we have related, not because we would reckon acts done by heretics valid (they are in fact invalid and without foundation and unsubstantial), but because we would explain that healing is not applied to converts from heresy in one way only, but according to the nature of the error: perfection and the cure of the disease being granted to some through baptism and ordination, to others through chrism, to others through their anathematizing the heresy in writing, and repudiating it and showing fruits of penitence. It is in fact absolutely necessary for us to follow the canonical precepts and regulations of the saintly bishops as medical directions given with understanding, and from them to apply to each man the cure p. 204.
suited to him. Therefore he also who has been received to communion by your love of God, if he scrupulously fulfil the prescribed time in the reforming practice of penitence and you bear witness to it, will be allowed the position of deacon by the orthodox bishops, upon presenting to them a written petition containing a confession of his sin and an anathema of the heresy. For the voice of a high-priest and bishop and his permission is a law of the Spirit, and full of power to turn the convert into another man, as is written about Saul when he heard the voice of the prophet Samuel, and went in the way that he ordered

[1] Ac. v. 36

him to go: and the sacred scripture speaks thus: "And it was so that, when he turned his shoulder to go from Samuel, God gave him a changed heart, and all these signs came upon him that day."[1] Those also who are in
p. 205. the rank of laymen, if they repudiate by anathema the Nestorian and Jewish heresy of the Diphysites, and by sincerely repenting place themselves within the bounds of the orthodox apostolic church, and are included among the sheep of the great God and chief shepherd Christ, will immediately cast from them everyone soever who is an alien, and will be invisibly adorned with the manifestations of the Holy Spirit. If a man on entering by night a house full of torches[2] is completely pervaded by the flashing light, who doubts that the church of the orthodox, which is full of the gifts of the Holy Spirit, causes the man who opens the eyes of a repentant heart to be pervaded by the light that is suprasensual and divine? The power of the true church assembled in a pure fashion in the Lord's name is so great that it even constitutes men who come to it prophets, men who have not joined the congregation in order to share in any divine gift, but in order to carry out a royal order. For in the first book of Kingdoms it is written thus: "And Saul sent messengers to take David. And they saw the church of the prophets, and Samuel was standing at their
p. 206. head. And the Spirit of God came upon the messengers of Saul, and they prophesy. And it was told

[1] 1 R. x. 9.

[2] λαμπάδα.

Saul and he sent other messengers and they also prophesy. And Saul again sent a third set of messengers, and they also prophesied."[1] If therefore at a time when the practices of the legal shadowy service prevailed the Holy Spirit granted such things to the assembly and the name of a church, what great and wonderful thing will it not do in the church that was bought by the divine blood of the Lamb and God, and has nothing shadowy in it, but the whole sun of righteousness flashing upon all the acts that are performed in it? For many other instances might have been added to those mentioned. At the very beginning when I was set over the Christ-loving city of the Antiochenes, and immediately, so to speak, upon my being raised to the episcopal throne (unworthily indeed, but still by God's p. 207. mercy), certain men who were infected with the self-created religion[2] of the Re-anointers, following a certain deceiver named Theodotus,[3] who unlawfully re-anointed converts from the Nestorian heresy to the orthodox faith, composed a petition consisting of uncanonical propositions,[4] and had this given to me as I was going out into the street by a certain man who was himself also a victim of their disease; and I have composed a certain short treatise against it. Accordingly out of respect for the love of teaching and the strictness of your religiousnesses I have thought it necessary to look

[1] 1 R. xix. 20, 21.

[2] *I.e.* ἐθελοθρησκεία (Col. i. 23).

[3] *Cf.* Zach. Rh. v. 5.

[4] προτάσεις.

for this and copy it out and send it you, in order that nothing bearing upon this subject[1] may remain unknown to you, so far as the power and the limited capacity that has fallen to the lot of my meanness extends. For we must "walk in the royal road," as it is written,[2] and "not turn aside to the right or to the left." For many, starting from considerations that are rather upon the right side than otherwise, have been led into excess, and so fallen into the very pit of destruction. For this reason
p. 208. also the text of the law commands that he that pursues after justice shall pursue it justly:[3] that is, know the principles of justice and be instructed in them when you pursue that which is just: and be free from all passion, and be in this respect a just seeker of justice, and restrain yourself on all sides, and stand within the bounds of justice. Many by the very fact of wishing to be just have become mentally drunk, and have injured justice through their justice which had the appearance of being strict. Whence also the wise Koheleth, or rather the teacher of wisdom (for the true Koheleth is Christ, the head of the church and the wisdom and the sublime and substantial power of God and the Father), checking excess, even if directed to the right side, gives admonition, saying, "Be not very righteous nor contrive superfluous wisdom, lest thou be astonied."[4] On all points therefore I praise your religiousnesses for having informed us of this present question, in order that you may wisely follow the precepts of the Holy

[1] ὑπόθεσις. [2] Nu. xx. 17. De. xvi. 20 [4] Ec. vii. 17.

Spirit: for it is written, "The wise turn not aside from the mouth of the Lord: but they reason in assemblies."[1] Accordingly, when a man is not so minded, p. 209. but, making his will law, does what comes into his mind, death is the penalty[2]. For he that said these things said also this: "Death lights upon the uninstructed."[3]

In answer to your other question I shrink and hesitate to say anything, and I tardily and reluctantly bring myself to answer, lest I be thought to be a cruel and harsh man, when I bring forward the strictness of the church tradition. For indeed this custom has prevailed in the holy churches up to the present day, I mean that after the reading of the holy revered book of the Gospels there should be a petition on behalf of the catechumens, one of the deacons proclaiming the names, and the presbyter thereupon offering a prayer applying to those whose names have been proclaimed, in order that they may receive the laver of regeneration and the communion of the holy mysteries, and that immediately afterwards another proclamation and prayer should follow on behalf of those that are possessed, in order that they also may be freed from the possession of evil spirits, and may receive the communion of the all-holy body and blood. Further, when the holy symbols that are consecrated in the mysterious sacrifice are about to be brought out into the church, and to be placed on the holy altar, the first of the deacons, look- p. 210. ing out of the door of the deacons' chamber, utters the

[1] Pr. xxiv. 7, 8. [2] ζημία. [3] Pr. xxiv. 8.

fearful and awful words, "No catechumen, no possessed person, no one that is incapable[1]," and so those that consecrate and those that have been consummated begin the ineffable sacred sacrifice, and send upwards the mysterious words. But I have nowhere found in the divine canons that such a distinction as this concerning those that are possessed is contained in them, the tenor of which is that if a man fights with a fierce demon, and is in the habit of assailing and attacking those who come in his way, and rends chains and fetters asunder like the man mentioned [in the Gospels . . . .] which[2] Paul the great also in writing to the Corinthians commands men to do, and to discern what is the power of the all-holy body, and to consider its greatness, and what the disposition[3] is in the heart of him who is to communicate in it. This is what he says: "But let a man examine himself, and so let him eat of the bread and drink of the cup. For he that eateth and drinketh when he is unworthy eateth and drinketh condemnation to himself, in that he hath not discerned the Lord's body. For this cause the sick and diseased among you are many, and there are many that sleep. For, if we judged ourselves, we should not be judged.
p. 211. But, being judged by the Lord, we are chastised, that we may not be condemned with the world:"[4] even as

[1] *I.e.* under penance; *cf.* Liturgy of Antioch ap. Brightman Liturgies, i. 471, 472.

[2] The subject of this fragment seems to show that it belongs to this letter. [3] διάθεσις. [4] 1 Co. xi. 28–32.

He that cares for our souls and is their benign instructor directs everything to this end, that He may not condemn us on the day on which He will judge the world and the earth in righteousness, in the last condemnation to which there is no end. Those that do not judge themselves, but communicate without fear in the holy body and blood He judges for a time, chastising them with sicknesses and with diseases that they may come to conversion and penitence. And some, even when they are incorrigible, He removes from life, in order that they may not be afflicted by endless torments of greater severity and greater bitterness in the world to come. Blessed therefore is he who has been visited here and been chastised as by an instructor and been moved to prepare for the better life, and does not "owing to his hardness and impenitent heart," as the Apostle says, "lay up" for himself "a store of wrath for the day of wrath, and for the revelation of the just judgment of God, who will render to every man according to his deeds."[1] Therefore he also who is possessed by an invasion of evil spirits must submit to the canon of the apostolic church, and endure the chastening with devoutness, and take upon him thoughts and expressions of thanksgiving and make confession to the Lord and say, "I have submitted to the Lord and made supplication to him": and He will assuredly have pity upon him (for "He is one that loveth mercy," as the prophet Micah says[2]), and will

[1] Ro. ii. 5, 6. [2] Mi. vii. 18.

p. 212. rebuke the operation of the evil spirit, and will deliver His creature. For a man to be contemptuously disposed, and to communicate in the sacraments or take part in the sacred ministry contrary to what is commanded makes the assault of man-hating spirits yet more fierce. This is also confirmed by the wise John who was bishop of Constantinople, in the sermon entitled "On the treason of Judas and on the Passover and on the institution of the mysteries, and concerning the principle that we should not retain anger," in that he wrote as follows: "For then also it was after Judas had received the oblation that the devil assailed him; not that he despised the Lord's body, but that he despised Judas on account of his presumption: in order that you may learn that it is especially those who communicate in the divine mysteries without being worthy that the devil constantly assails and attacks, as he attacked Judas then. For privileges benefit those who are worthy: but, when men enjoy them undeservedly, they expose them to greater punishment. And these things I do not say in order to frighten, but in order to secure."[1] As I said before, the intention of the disciplinary regulations of the canons is to preserve the visible appearance of the church blameless. For this reason they forbade those also who are possessed by an invasion
p. 213. of demons to communicate in the holy mysteries: but invisible and secret afflictions [they left] to the

[1] P.G. xlix. 380.

conscience of each man. . . . .

. . . .

61. . . . . 519-25.
a law-court, or to cry out or to annoy in return those who annoyed him, or to insult in return those who insulted him, or to bring an action against them for the insult to him, similarly and much more is it unbecoming for him who has just received the high-priestly chrism upon the crown of his head, and from whom the sweet savour therefrom is newly breathing, to involve himself in any of the said matters. Do not think to yourself, because the man who was ordained high-priest is not clad in white raiment, that he is without the garments that are suprasensual and shine more brightly than the brilliancy of the sun, and are as much better than those of men who have just been baptized as a high-priest is greater than one who is among the people, and as a shepherd is higher than a sheep.

And again after other things. But you say that the devout brother Joseph told you such-and-such a thing about the devout brother John, and the devout father Zacharias such-and-such a thing about another topic.[1] But know that in every matter it is not the word of one man that is needed, but that of two or three witnesses. For the sacred law says of everyone soever who is tried, whether he be good or whether he p. 214.
be evil, that "under two or under three witnesses he shall die that dieth: he shall not die under one wit-

[1] κεφάλαιον.

ness:[1] and again, "One witness shall not continue to testify against a man, [in all] iniquity and in all sin and in all sinfulness soever that he commit. At the mouth of two witnesses, and at the mouth of three witnesses shall every word be established."[2] I have used these arguments not in order to show that your religiousness is lying (I am convinced that you wrote as you heard): but in order to establish the fact that, according to church regulations and the precepts of the holy fathers, and the laws of the God-inspired scripture, I cannot upon this report pronounce a sentence of censure or of condemnation against anyone, while I am far away. Your love of God ought therefore to have devoted that evening to thoughts of patience: and on the next day taken with you in the morning the saintly bishops the lord Constantine and the lord Victor, as in fact you actually did, and [with] all gentleness and humility, [and with] God . . . . also present . . . . at the discussion [first described] the circumstances of the annoyance that the deaconess and archimandritess Heracliana inflicted upon you, and the insults which, as you write, were levelled against you by brother John; and thus your sanctity would have judged, with
p. 215. the awful tribunal of Christ, before which we shall all stand, before your eyes, whether it was right for your love of God on account of the annoyance that you justly felt to remove those sisters from the monastery of the religious Heracliana as persons who were suffer-

[1] De. xvii. 6. [2] *Id.*, xix. 15.

ing injury or not, and what method of treatment ought to be devised (?) for the affair in order to remedy the injury; and the use of this method would have been decreed; and besides this fitting punishment would also have fallen upon brother John, inasmuch as he would have been shown by proofs to be an utterer of insults, and a man who is living an unchaste and indiscriminate life. If these things had been thus decided by discussion, and made known to my meanness, I would without any hesitation have confirmed them, seeing that they would have been carried out in accordance with the custom of the holy churches, and in accordance with the rules of the monastic life.

And again after other things. But, since these things are thus recorded and supported by evidence, if anything displeasing to God be done in secret, know that it is not possible that until the end . . . .

. . . .

62. . . . . 519–38.

. . . .

And it seems to me that it was owing to this moderation of character and humility of mind that the God-inspired scripture in Omissions named Moses "the p. 216.
man of God," the words of the context being as follows: "And Moses, the man of God. And his sons were called to the observance[1] of Levi."[2] As to your[3] saying, "We were afraid on account of the present

[1] The translator therefore read φυλακὴν for φυλήν.

[2] 1 Pa. xxiii. 14.

[3] Fem. pl.; so throughout.

time of confusion and persecution, lest we and the places in which we live should lack bishops to ordain," as far as the ordination of a presbyter or of a male deacon, by whom the bloodless sacrifice is of necessity performed, is concerned, this plea would have been good. But in the case of a female deaconess, especially in monasteries, ordination is received not so much for the sake of the requirements of the mysteries, but for the sake of honour only (for the deaconesses in the cities are in the habit of ministering to the divine laver of regeneration in the case of females who are baptized). These things I have been compelled to repeat owing to my wish and prayer that in accordance with your high and praiseworthy character you may do everything in a lawful manner and, as it is written in Proverbs and in the Apostle, "provide things honest not only before the Lord but also before men,"[1] so that, in accordance with the testimony of our God and Saviour Jesus, "your light may shine before men" and "they may glorify your Father in heaven,"[2] and we ourselves may justly boast of you. And, now that these words have been thus spoken, we pray that God may grant a good ending to the things which have once in whatever way been done by you, and may cover them with the abundance of His graciousness. *Not the end.*

[1] Pr. iii. 4; 2 Co. viii. 21. [2] Mt. v. 16.

p. 217.

63. *Of the same to Misael the deacon.* (*From those after banishment, from the 9th book the 43rd letter.*) 537.

I received the letter of your religiousness, which was forwarded to me from Alexandria, from the devout Andrew the reader on the eighth of July. *And after other things.* The holy Basil also, the teacher of truth, says in his ascetic treatise that he who is entrusted with the duty of ministering to the needs of a monastery, even if it be the archimandrite, ought not to use or spend any of the property of the brotherhood on any pious object, for example on the support of the poor and needy or on the ransoming of captives. Therefore neither would the case of the saintly man, though it seems to be a matter of piety, have given you a right to do anything without my consent, if you are certain from the laws and from the will[1] which left the legacy[2] that it is mine. For you must excuse me from adopting the honorary expressions used by friends or by men who are otherwise on familiar terms with one another, "My things are yours," and, "You are my lord, lord both of my own person and of what I possess." For the subject of the present argument is the true state of the facts. Moreover also the saintly man[3] does not need a gift from us, seeing p. 218.
that he has the serene queen, who will provide him

[1] διάθεσις. [2] ληγᾶτον. [3] Marg. "he speaks of Theodosius."

if he wish even with more than he needs, and now he has all the orthodox also on account of his attested steadfastness in the matter of the confession of the faith. These things I have written for the sake of the principles of the evangelic laws, and for the sake of preserving a blameless conscience. If it were not so, I reckon things once given by you just as if they had been given by me.

And after other things. As to the impious Sergius, who is called Bar Fathya[1] and has become broad in impiety, so far am I from saying that it was by my advice that he was ordained deacon that I even anathematize him and the man who, if even in this he speaks truth, ordained him : the one for unlawfully sleeping with his father's wife or concubine, and the other for daring to perform ordinations without witnesses in other men's cities which do not belong to him at all, without an invitation and on his own authority, and not even without price but for filthy lucre. Under the same anathema lies also Anatolius, who after ordination to the diaconate has married a second time and is godless in his doctrines,
p. 219. even if it is not stated by us, and Podolirius[2] who has taught his children to play the harp and dance, and has made them serve the devil, and has fallen under the divine canons of the apostles. To the same anathema those also are liable who cause confusion

[1] *I.e.* son of the broad. Probably a rendering of some Greek name (Platys?).

[2] *Sic.*

besides these, and imagine vain things against the orthodox faith, like those who once "imagined vain things against the Lord and against his Anointed,"[1] and fell from His glory. For these too by always reckoning the belly and the passions that are subject to the belly as a god inflicted a stain and a blot upon us by being numbered with the orthodox. Therefore they must plead not to us but to God, whose name they are profaning among the nations as Isaiah and Paul say.[2]

And after other things. But I was much distressed that the serene queen presumes to say such grievous, not to say blasphemous, things against the holy fathers in respect of doctrines which she does not understand, and mocks at the holy Alexander the archbishop, who is one of the prelates of the holy synod at Nicæa, and father of the apostolic preacher Athanasius, on the ground that even in the theology of the Trinity he termed person "nature," and jeers at him as one of those who practise manual crafts, a coppersmith for instance or a carpenter of the name of Alexander, or as she says by way of accusation an p. 220.
advocate of the treasure-chambers.[3] Let her then mock and jeer at the other saintly Alexander also, who was in the same times bishop of Constantinople, and by stretching out his hands all night and praying brought it about that, when the impious Arius was going to communicate hypocritically with the orthodox, his entrails fell through his belly and he gave up the

[1] Ps. ii. 1, 2. [2] Is. lii. 5; Ro. ii. 24. [3] I.e. *advocatus fisci.*

ghost; if the fact that a man is called Alexander is a jest, and an occasion and subject[1] for jeering. What are we to do about these things, except be silent and grieve our heart, and ask God to have mercy upon our many lawlessnesses? For, though much might have been said in answer to these things, it is better for us to be silent. As to the mischievous words that the heretics invent, the expressions of the holy fathers show what they are, blinding as they do like some lightning-flash their keen eyes, and enlightening the minds of the orthodox and understanding, while the uninstructed and unlearned see that God is glorified and admired among His saints, as David says in song,[2] for the things at which they jest and against which they blaspheme. I speak the truth and do not lie when I say that, since I wrote the treatise "Against the Grammarian,"[3] there has been no one among
p. 221. the believers who had a high or moderate or small share in divine knowledge who was not astonished when he found such expressions of the holy fathers collected there, some expressed at length others in few words, and stopping the mouth of the blaspheming heretics, who plot against the truth itself. From what you now say, that the serene queen has not shrunk from saying such presumptuous things against the holy fathers, I certainly imagine that she has also spurned and despised, as vain trifling and superfluous futility,

---

[1] ὑπόθεσις.

[2] Ps. lxxxviii. 8.

[3] Add. 17,154; *cf.* Zach. Rh. vii. 10.

my little treatise on the question whether our Lord and God Jesus Christ should be said to be from two substances even as from two natures, which she thought good to accept when it was copied by you in large letters, or through fear of the king's laws which were put forth against my writings has not dared to accept it. I wrote to you at that time from Chios and to the magnificent and Christ-loving chamberlain Julian to give it to be copied: but you wrote nothing at all to me upon these matters. He who writes an answer should reply to all the points contained in the letter. *Not the end.*

II. Second section.[1] About his ordination before episcopacy; and about the precedence of bishops and another doubtful point regarding them; and about men who give themselves out as bishops and ordain; and about the proper ordination of bishops. p. 222.

---

1. *Of the same to the patricians.* (*From those before episcopacy, from the 3rd book the 5th letter.*) 508-11.

As the brightness of the stars brings comfort to those who in the depth of night raise their looks towards heaven, so it is good for us also, whose

[1] τίτλος.

mind's eye is darkened by the darkness of sorrow, to look towards you the rational stars of the sacred Senate.[1] If we are allowed to enjoy your genial splendour, all the cloud of despondency will pass away, and we shall certainly see the sun also which is surrounded by you shining gently upon us as at hot noonday. It has come to the ears of our
p. 223. worthlessness that our pious Christ-loving king believed that some of us without having priestly rank are officiating as priests with profane hands and handling the sacraments. Such reports it is the practice of slanderers to put forth about us: who, being unable to accuse the orthodoxy of our faith for which we were persecuted, betake themselves to such unholy futilities. But our acts are known to everyone, even if we ourselves keep silent. Although we are sinners, yet we are not unversed in the divine scriptures, nor have we an uninstructed mind with regard to them (I forbear to say that we make these our meditation by night and by day, as we are commanded[2]). Trying therefore as we do to direct our own life by them, we know that all who coveted the priestly functions without being in the position of priests suffered sudden death. Such were Dathan and Abiram and the company of Korah: who wished to usurp the high-priestly office of Moses and Aaron, and dared to burn incense, and the earth opened and swallowed some of them up,

[1] σύγκλητος βουλή.

[2] Josh. i. 8.

while others were consumed by the strange fire. Another man, because he presumed to touch the sacred ark with profane hand when it leaned over and was about to be dashed to the ground, was immediately struck lifeless. And what of Uzziah the p. 224.
king? Is it not the fact that, because he inconsiderately dared to be called a priest, he was smitten with the scab of leprosy between his eyes before he passed the sacred barrier[1] or veil, and was thenceforth ashamed even to reign? How then could we who through mercy devote ourselves to the study of such teachings, and so know that there was power even in the legal shadowy service, have presumed to officiate as priests with unconsecrated hands at the heavenly sacrifice, which even to angels is inaccessible, but out of benignance has been made accessible to the priests only, because they typify Christ? For it is in truth He who down to the present time offers Himself every day on our behalf to God and the Father. Those who minister in the new covenant[2] do not offer any new sacrifice upon the altar, but celebrate the memory of that one, in which Christ, God the Word the high-priest, the priesthood, the new and glorious victim, and noble oblation preparative for immortal life, offered Himself. In fact the wise Paul also in his epistle to the Hebrews says of Christ, "By one offering He hath perfected them that are sanctified:"[3] and again, "So also Christ, having been once offered to bear the sins

[1] κάγκελον.

[2] διαθήκη.

[3] He. x. 14.

of many, shall appear a second time without sin, to those who look for Him for salvation through faith." [1] That Christ's mystery is inaccessible even to the p. 225. sublime hosts Isaiah the loud trumpet of the prophets bears witness who said that one of the suprasensual and immaterial hosts of the seraphs took a coal with the tongs and not in his hand, and laid it on his lips and said, "This shall purge thy sins." [2] That the coal signifies the one Christ made out of two elements, of the Godhead I mean and of the manhood which are each perfect, undoubtedly does not escape your God-loving excellencies. Holding therefore to such right principles, in order to cause perfect confidence in what we say, we lay ourselves under the direst curse, to fall from the glory of the Holy Trinity and not attain to the hope promised to Christians, if we are conscious in ourselves that any such presumptuous deed has been committed by our fathers or is being committed. If anyone presumes to lay hands upon the priesthood without having received the sacred ordination lawfully and in accordance with the apostolic canons, let him be anathema, and let him be ranked with men that rob a sanctuary and lie in wait at altars.[3] The other slander also we cast from us and assert that no one who has been admitted to the clergy in the churches has been re-ordained among us. Wherefore we even p. 226. place under anathema the man who re-ordains these,

[1] *Id.* ix. 28. [2] Is. vi. 6, 7. [3] *I.e.* ἱερόσυλοι and βωμολόχοι.

or says that they must be re-ordained. But, if anyone after he has been admitted to the clergy has turned his eye towards the solitary mode of life, and, being trained in the toilsome exercises of philosophy, and desiring to know how to bear contempt for Christ's sake, has debarred himself for a time from the ministry, this is not re-ordination (far be it!), but a philosophic and divine exercise which renders the priest more worthy of reverence. It is in fact the custom of our fathers to look to the soul's profit only, and, when men have once taken upon themselves to practise philosophy, whether they be priests or whether they be kings, to lead them on through the performance of humble services, in order that by trampling upon pride they may imitate Him who humbled Himself for our salvation and became flesh and took the form of a slave. For the correct definition of philosophy is this, that a man imitate God as much as possible. Therefore, now that you know these things, we beg your glorious noble eminences to convey them to the ears of our Christ-loving triumphant king. For it is not just that, when we are near and able to give satisfactory answers to the slanders against us, that we should be condemned by default as if we were absent. *The end.*

p. 227.

519-38. 2. *Of the same to John and John the presbyters.* (*From those after banishment, from the* 1*st book the* 6*th letter.*)

Your holinesses' letter, which was brought me by Zenobius the devout deacon, has refreshed me greatly, and has been to me, as in the words of the proverb, "as cool water that relieveth a thirsty soul."[1] *And after other things.* As to what you say about those who are residing in Byzantium, the report that has been received is true, that they contended about precedence. In fact at an earlier time also they discussed this doubtful point, and the proper regulation[2] was given. Now however, when they are outside the phantasy[3] of worldly sleep, they ought not to have contended as with a shadow and seen dreams. But may the hateful passion of jealousy and envy perish from among men, a passion that goes down with a man even to Hades itself and is a thing unendurable! For this reason the God-inspired scripture says, "Wrath is merciless and anger sharp, but nothing endureth jealousy."[4] For both the merciless wrath and the sharp anger eat away and destroy those against whom they are whetted: but still it is sometimes possible for us to assuage them and turn them aside, by lapse of time and by methods of treatment and by gifts. But jealousy there is nothing than can endure. This
p. 228. passion knows one relief, the destruction of the man

[1] Pr. xxv. 25. [2] τύπος. [3] φαντασία. [4] Pr. xxvii. 4.

who is its object, and his ruin: and in the same fashion also the death of the man himself who is jealous: especially that of the soul before that of the body. For the very wise book of Job says, "Jealousy slayeth him that is in error."[1] Such annoyances I received from the two aforesaid men: and He who came down from on high and humbled Himself for our sake and said, "My peace I give unto you, my tranquillity I leave unto you,"[2] breathed upon them and extinguished their gall, and even caused them wholly to disappear. Do not wonder if these strove about precedence. Such things indeed happened even in former times. When in old days Helladius succeeded to the see of the men of Cæsarea after the great and renowned Basil, a man who lived a virtuous life and was worthy of such a succession, and was one of the holy men of the synod of the hundred and fifty, Cappadocia having been divided into two, Theodore, a man praiseworthy both for faith and for character, was bishop of the other metropolis (this was Tyana): and under him among others was Bosporius, a good man and one who had reached such a high standard of holiness that even his p. 229.
grave performs miracles down to the present day. But, though they were both of such a character and so highly exalted in virtue, they strove with one another about some contemptible claim of right in their parish, and fell into great and long rivalry: and they had the two Gregories, he of Nyssa siding with Helladius and

[1] Job v. 5. [2] John xiv. 27.

he of Nazianzus with Theodore, and Bosporius the renowned, divided in sympathies, and like armed men bringing help to the generals when they engaged in battle, and writing letters in opposition to one another. If then those towers of the church and men of heavenly minds were convicted of sometimes walking upon earth, what will a man say of ourselves the gnats, who are ever flying over the sores and mire of passions and feeding on them? Nor yet at this must one wonder, I mean that one of the very men who have been mentioned now uses humble words, saying, "It is against the things done at Chalcedon, not against the actual
p. 230. synod itself, that we must put forth a sentence and anathema." For Liberius, the bishop of Rome, resisted Constantius even to blood, on behalf of Athanasius the apostolic preacher of the orthodox faith, and went out to the figurative *stadium*, and readily allowed himself to be carried into exile: and at last, bent by the long continuance of the sojourn in the place of exile, he gave way, and yielded to the violence of the time. Hosius also the bishop of Corduba (a little city so named), who had always been arrayed on the side of the orthodox, owing to his extreme old age and advanced time of life, was overcome at Nice in Thrace, and submitted to compulsion. And Athanasius the champion[1] of the truth in word and in deed, a man of practised skill in doing service, who discharges the rational shafts against enemies with understanding,

[1] ἀγωνιστής.

both in epistles and in treatises against the Ariomanitæ calls Hosius "of honourable old age,"[1] and mentions him with distinction: while in respect of the contests undergone by Liberius he praises and extols the man; saying not a word of what happened to them under violence, but like a wise man passing rapidly over it p. 231. with closed eyes, as the saying is. Let us also therefore, inasmuch as sacred contests lie before us, follow the spiritual captains, and in respect of actions on the right side, both be ourselves edified and edify others thereby, in order that the others also may be strengthened: but human actions let us pass rapidly over. For we are mortal and weak, and we are put under compulsion and led by force by spirits of wickedness. Let us pray therefore that the details of our weakness be not greatly exposed. But you for your part have the power of sharing the contest with everyone through your prayers. *Not the end.*

3. *Of the same to the orthodox in Emesa.* (*From those* 518-9.
after banishment, from the 2*nd book the* 93*rd letter.*)[2]

Men often think that time is bringing them new and unwonted events. Nevertheless they are not such as are wholly without similar instances in times that have already passed. This is confirmed by Koheleth who

[1] Ap. c. Ar. 44 (?). This is in a letter of the Synod of Sardica.

[2] A comparison with ix. 1 seems to show that this letter was written very soon after banishment.

says, "There is nothing new under the sun."[1] Many
indeed have desired the priesthood in an unhallowed
manner; of which unlawful thought an instance was
provided in time past by Dathan and Abiram, and the
company of Korah who rose against Moses and Aaron,
the first priests under the shadowy law. A scion of
p. 232. this impious action and of this audacious deed is this
also which has just been reported to me in the desert,
where I am dwelling unseen for the sake of the com-
mon hope and substance of our salvation, which is
the orthodox faith. I learn that a certain Gregory
and Isaiah, who register their fathers' house the one
in Pontus, the other in Armenia, have appeared in
the countries of the East and are falsely and lyingly
ascribing to themselves the great name and the func-
tions of the episcopate: and it is reported that their
mad practices do not extend to words only: but
Gregory in the great distinguished Christ-loving city
of the Antiochenes, and Isaiah in the illustrious believ-
ing metropolis of the Emesenes, have laid their pre-
sumptuous and illegal hand upon certain men, and by a
mockery as in a play will create certain men ridiculous
priests for filthy lucre; like those whom Jeroboam the
rebel created, after he had led the ten tribes away from
the lawful service which was established through Moses
the great, and fashioned golden calves, and by one and
the same creation instituted at the same time both the
p. 233. hateful thing and the falsely-named hierophants[2] of

[1] Ec. i. 9.

[2] *Marzane* = μῦσται.

the creation itself. Gregory, I learn, has created a fraud more plausible than that of Isaiah ; having in fact stated of himself that he is bishop of Diocæsarea which is situated in the Pontic diocese, and that he left his throne on account of the sound faith : which, if true, would be worthy of crowns, and of all praise that is warranted by the spiritual laws : and, to speak plainly, a thing preparative for the kingdom of heaven according to the voice of the Lord that cannot lie which cries in the Gospels, "Blessed are they which have been persecuted for righteousness' sake for theirs is the kingdom of heaven."[1] But Isaiah's elaboration is, I learn, twice as abominable : and it has been so badly concocted that, even if the foolish tale were established, he would have no confirmation whatever for his position nor any plausibility. Certain men in Egypt told me that he says he is a bishop, but, when he alleges ordination to have been performed over him, he produces no evidence or proof, names no city, and says that it was performed by one man, and by him when he was drawing his last breath and lying dead. For, when he kept perversely lying and was asked for proof of what he was saying, he came down to this as the sum of the allegation and tripped himself up. This is in fact established by the sacred text which says, "He that is incautious with his lips in that he is perverse shall be tripped up."[2] Who p. 234.
is there who is reckoned among Christians to whom it is not manifest that these things stand outside all

[1] Mt. v. 10. [2] Pr. x. 8.

canonical order and the apostolic church? Indeed from the very beginning those who were disciples and eye-witnesses and ministers of the Word Himself divided the bishops among cities, and to each church as to a spiritual bride figuratively united the bishop as a bridegroom. A witness of this is the divine Paul who writes to Titus and says, "For this cause left I thee in Crete that thou shouldest set in order the things that are wanting, and appoint presbyters in every city as I commanded thee." Here he calls bishops presbyters: for indeed after saying, "In order that thou shouldest appoint presbyters in every city," he went on further to say, "For the bishop must be blameless, as the steward of God."[1] This the holy John also, who was bishop of Constantinople, interpreted in this way when he wrote as follows about Titus: "This man was highly approved among those who were with Paul: and, if not, he would not have entrusted the island to him in its entirety, nor have commanded him to supply the things that were wanting ('in order that thou shouldest set in order the
p. 235. things that are wanting'): he would not have entrusted him with the selection of so many bishops, if it had not been that he had great confidence in the man."[2] The apostles also divided the peoples by the lots of the Holy Spirit: and each of them took possession of the inheritance that was given to him, and was contented with it: and the gift of it was made to him by inspira-

[1] Tit. i. 5, 7.

[2] P.G. lxii. 663.

tion from above. This gift the singing prophet compared to the wings of a dove that are covered with silver and her feathers superbly decorated with gold; and he foretold that this grace would be given them openly and in actual deeds, in that he addresses his words to them thus, "If ye lie among the lots, there there are the wings of a dove that are covered with silver, and her feathers with the yellowness of gold":[1] the words manifestly showing this, that, if each apostle had not been satisfied with the lot that fell to him and shown regard for order, the Holy Spirit would not have bountifully bestowed upon them illustrious powers of working signs and wonders, and teaching that shone after the fashion of silver, and the steadfastness in sufferings which gold shows when tried in the fire of the furnace. But the excellent Isaiah does not fear to give himself out as holding a bishopric not obtained by lot and irregular and without a city. Who has seen a marriage-chamber of an unnamed bride, and a foul bridegroom without a consort, or rather one who becomes everything to himself, as the nature of his fiction requires? I hear that those who after the p. 236.
fashion of some brute beast have adhered to his error, three or four wicked creatures, bring forward a canon also to substantiate their fraud which is without substance and full of all absurdity. This they also say is a canon of Simon the Cananæan, and it has never prevailed in the holy churches and been accepted by holy

[1] Ps. lxvii. 14.

synods, or been named in them at all. How could it have been, when the holy canons once for all enact that the ordination of a bishop must not be performed under any other conditions by him who has the right to ordain except when all the bishops of the same province[1] take part in the solemn function, or, if they are not all present, at any rate there shall be no smaller number than three, and the others also shall give their *psephisma* by their letters, even if they are absent in body?[2] For in ecclesiastical regulations enactments carefully made at a later time in the churches allow no play to those of ancient date. For
p. 237. example Cyprian the divine among bishops, who adorned the chief throne of Africa with all excellencies, but above all with a crown of martyrdom, once assembled a synod of the saintly bishops under him and ruled that converts from heresy must not be accepted, unless they have received the baptism given by the orthodox. And in modern times, now that the high-priests who fed the churches in the West and in the East, as well as the great and holy synod of the three hundred and eighteen, have discussed the quality of heresies, and enacted that we ought not in the case of all of them to accept penitents through baptism, no one presumes contrary to this conclusion to apply baptism to those who come from all heresies, as seemed right at an earlier time to Cyprian: but, if anyone contrary to the law which has prevailed shall

---

[1] ἐπαρχία.

[2] Mansi ii. 669.

presume to re-baptize, he will fall within the grasp of the canons as having performed unlawful actions. The bishop also of the city renowned for its orthodox faith of the city[1] of the Alexandrines was in old times appointed by presbyters. But in modern times, in accordance with the canon which has prevailed every- p. 238.
where, the solemn institution of their bishop is performed by bishops: and no one makes light of the accurate practice that prevails in the holy churches and recurs to the earlier condition of things, which has given way to the later clear and accurate, deliberate and spiritual injunctions.[2] However, if agreeable, we will also adduce the canon that is given out as having been enacted by Simon the Cananæan, in order that everyone may learn that Isaiah's partners in the idle fiction are stirring up destruction against themselves, as the common saying is. It is said to be as follows: "I also, Simon the Cananæan, command you by how many the bishop ought to be ordained. A bishop should be ordained by two or by three bishops. But, if anyone be ordained by one bishop, let both him and the man who ordained him be deprived. But, if necessity arise for him to be ordained by one, since a large number cannot come, because there is a persecution or some other cause, let him bring a p. 239.
psephisma of authority from several bishops."[3] Where then are we to place the fictitious ordination of Isaiah,

[1] Misunderstanding of πόλεως τῆς Ἀλεξανδρέων.

[2] See Journ. of Theol. St. ii. 612, iii. 278. [3] Const. Ap. viii. 27.

which passes all plausibility? Who are the bishops who confirmed for him the ordination that was performed by one as he says? or where are those who made the *psephisma* about him? It is known to everyone that the apostles made all their enactments through the Holy Spirit, and saw the future like the present through the illumination of the heavenly light from above. Therefore it seems that Isaiah's ordination escaped the notice of Simon the Cananæan, and the fact that it alone was to be devoid of bishops to make a *psephisma* about him, and to confirm that which was lame and imperfect. This is an absurdity, and a piece of silly trifling: nay rather it is a fit subject for sorrow, and fraught with tears. For how will even the spirits of the saints refrain from sighing when they see the high priesthood, which is awful even in the sight of the heavenly powers themselves, turned into a mockery? For of such a kind are the mysteries to which we summon, which, as Peter the chosen one of the apostles wrote, even "the angels desire to look into."[1] What need is there of many words, when the very devices of Isaiah the stony man, who has taken to him all the madness of Satan, show the demon-like nature of the act? He has indeed refuted his impiety which he falsely reported of himself by means of another
p. 240. impiety, adding iniquity to his iniquity according to the saying of the Psalmist in the Psalms.[2] For he did not even stay his presumptuous and unholy hand at

[1] 1 Pe. i. 12.

[2] Ps. lxviii. 28.

the name of deacons and of presbyters, but he assigns bishops also and archbishops to peoples and to cities, after the manner of the giants of the fable who sprang from the earth. And "let so-and-so," he says, "be archbishop of Egypt: and so-and-so of Pamphylia: and another of Palestine": and, since he lacks instruments for such madness, I have learned that he even collects men for himself from the crossroads, some blind men some lepers, some men with other bodily afflictions or suffering from disease. When I say this, I do not put forward the infirmities of the body as something shameful (the one real sickness and disease is the sin of the soul and falling away on our part from God), but I am desirous of showing the folly of the lunatic, how he is eager to lay his unholy and all-presumptuous hand even upon irrational things, if one may so speak, if the fatuity of men fail him. The holy Basil also in his letters mentions such roving pseudo-bishops as having been foolishly instituted by the foolish Apollinaris, writing thus: "Is not the great mystery of religion made a laughing-stock, in that bishops are going about without p. 241.
people and clergy, carrying about the bare name only, and doing no such right action as tends to the extension of the gospel of our salvation?"[1]; so the spirit of error, which uttered much nonsense in Apollinaris and in the heretics who resemble him, but was deaf and dumb, as the Gospel says,[2] was in Isaiah

[1] Ep. 265. 2. [2] Mk. ix. 25.

and knew how to do uncanonical acts. Many other things might be said to refute the illegal fraud and this irrational madness. But, since the greatness of the unseemly and unstable abomination reaches to absurdity, it is a very superfluous thing to extend the discussion unnecessarily. What synod of saintly orthodox bishops has accepted this? Who has not closed his ears and refused to endure even so much as the bare mention of this unlawful report? In what other country did not the gentle Isaiah deceive, or to what place did he not betake himself, as we may hear those that know relate? Did he not move his erring steps to Egypt seeing that he has no stability, but as Jeremiah the prophet says loved to move his feet[1]? did he not
p. 242. betake himself to Pamphylia, boasting and lying and saying that he was called to this illegal episcopate by Leontius the saintly old hermit, who practised the philosophic life in the wilderness? for on the contrary he was actually anathematized by him by word of mouth, as all who dwell in that country testify. Did he not also come to the great Christ-loving city of Alexander, having been driven to it, like some ship without a helmsman, by the stormy waves of error; and, after he had been rejected by all, form the plan, as he in fact said, of confirming the fiction regarding him by supposed signs, and setting himself to imitate Christ, and fast forty days continuously, in order to raise a dead boy who lay like meat that has been dried

[1] Jer. xiv. 10.

and thrown into an earthenware vessel; but, when the greater part of the forty days had passed, he was sorely tried by the lack of food, which was broken by bread taken by stealth, though he hypocritically pretended not to have tasted anything; while the dead boy's father was beginning to mourn and weep at having been disappointed of his hope, and was crying aloud and wailing bitterly and after the manner of a rustic (he was a gardener); but the body having become putrid filled the house with noisome corruption and a deadly smell, so that the pretended bishop, simulated p. 243.
faster, and false miracle-worker was in danger of being delivered to the fire, seeing that his hateful conduct had been exposed, if it had not been that he hid himself and escaped from the hands of those who sought to inflict a just vengeance upon him for the drunkenness of his mind? Is inquiry therefore needed in the case of such men, who from the declaration[1] of our Saviour himself have the confutation which plainly says of false shepherds like them, "By their fruits ye shall know them"[2]? If "the less is blessed by the greater,"[3] as the wise Paul says, let us examine as a proposition who it was who gave Isaiah the fictitious ordination. Was it one who has the right of ordaining bishops and, being a metropolitan, knows also the prayer for the appointment of high-priests? or, if as a concession we grant this point also, how does a bishop of a metropolis give a man who is ordained by him authority to institute

[1] ἀπόφασις. [2] Mt. vii. 16 [3] He. vii. 7.

archbishops among peoples and cities, as in fables and
dreams? If, as he says, bishop Epiphanius of saintly
memory[1] was actually drawing his last breath and giv-
ing up the ghost, a man who was not bishop of a
p. 244. metropolis, but of one of the cities under a metropolis,
and gave him the hand of ordination at the moment of
death, and never finished the ordination such as it was,
what are we to say of such a prayer? and how is it not
a matter for tears, if Paul in speaking to the Corinthians
about all prayer says, "I will pray with my spirit, I
will pray also with my understanding,"[2] while Isaiah's
institutor uttered the prayer which is, if one may so
say, higher and more solemn than all prayers, I mean
that which institutes high-priests, with faltering tongue
and indistinct and feeble voice, when he had not even
ordinary intelligent consciousness, and heard it repeated
from a book like a small boy who goes to school, and
each word[3] was pronounced and lisped to him by those
standing round him, since they elaborate this also as
part and parcel of the snare and fraud? All the details
of this elaborate play and of the case[4] show weakness
and lack of substance, but set the saintly bishop Epi-
phanius free from calumny, who departed blamelessly
to the Lord, and, when he stands before the judgment-
seat that does not respect persons on the last day, will
have no knowledge of what the prayer of the ordination
p. 245. of a bishop is, and by the sentence of the just Judge
will send those who calumniate him to the fire that is

[1] *Cf.* vit. Sev. p. 26 l. 37.
[2] 1 Co. xiv. 15.
[3] λέξεις.
[4] ὑπόθεσις.

not quenched, and the wicked Isaiah to the outer darkness, with those that are "clad in strange apparel," as one of the prophets said.[1] Why should one repeat the whole story? It has been told me that he has reached such a height of madness as even to entitle himself "high-priest of high-priests," and even "apostle" also, and thereby to show everyone that he has received the evil spirit of Montanus and of Mani. For in fact those also named themselves apostles, and presumed to exalt themselves to the title of Paraclete which cannot be shared by any creature, and fitly belongs to Christ only and to the Holy Spirit; imitating Satan the chief of the rebel host, who in ancient times said, "I will exalt myself to heaven, and above the stars of heaven will I set my throne,"[2] and is also expected through Antichrist, as Paul the speaker of divine things foretold, "to sit in the temple of God and make it appear concerning himself that he is God."[3] And yet, after those stupid unlearned advocates of the error have gone through all these things which show the artificial nature of the fiction, they presume, I hear, to cite, as if the imaginary ordination of Isaiah were valid, the action that was taken in the case of Gregory the Miracle-worker, I mean how Phædimus who ordained this man p. 246.
hunted him by the power of prayer when he was fleeing from the burden of the bishopric, and when absent and at a distance uttered a prayer, so that even when absent he was involved in the chains of prayer, and

[1] Zeph. i. 8. [2] Is. xiv. 13, 14. [3] 2 Th. ii. 4.

was caught in the nets of the Spirit from which there is no escape, and hastened to him who was lawfully pursuing him, and thus underwent and received all the legal requirements of ordination, and did not stop at the prayer made at a distance, as is thought by the men who are bereft of intelligence and do not understand what they read. A witness of this is Gregory, who wrote his history, the brother in blood and in the Spirit and in the office of the high-priesthood of the great Basil, and bishop of Nyssa, who wrote as follows: "For this reason Phædimus having been by some specially divine impulse roused to the task before him, paying no regard to the intervening space by which he was separated from Gregory (seeing he was three days' journey distant from him), but, looking to God and saying that he himself was seen by God at that hour in the same way as he was, in place of a hand applies the spoken word to Gregory, dedicating to God a man who was absent in body, and allotting
p. 247. him to a city which down to those times had, it so happened, been held in the error of idols, so that, while those who dwelt in the city itself and in its neighbourhood were without number, there were not found more than seventeen who had received the word of faith. Having thus therefore received the yoke by force, and all the legal requirements having afterwards been performed over him, and having asked the man who proclaimed the priesthood over him for a short time to reflect upon the exact character of the mystery, he no longer thought it right for him, as the Apostle

said, to 'attend to blood and flesh,' but asked God that a revelation of the secrets might be made to him."[1] You see he has clearly shown that the prayer made at a distance only stopped his course of flight, but all the legal requirements were performed over him after he had hastened to him who consecrated him, and nothing whatever was lacking. At the same time it has certainly been admitted that, since Phædimus was head of the metropolis of the men of Amasia, that he had his bishops close by him, and with them pursued Gregory. For, when he pursued, he pursued promptly: so that, when he had caught the quarry, he immediately performed the ordination. Accordingly he had the bishops standing round him, and taking part with him in the prayer also that was made over the divine Gregory at a distance. But it seems p. 248.
ridiculous for us to pass beyond the proper limits in considering the silly arguments of those deceivers, and to go on to refute arguments that are feeble and have no substance, which some intelligent and devout hermits repeated to me in Egypt as having been invented by one of Isaiah's deceivers. To these I also said, "The saintly bishop Epiphanius we ourselves committed to the grave in our monastery[2] in Palestine: and of these follies and futilities we have a clear written refutation. For indeed at the very end of his life he made a will,[3] in which he appointed count Eusebius the Alexandrine of magnificent

[1] P.G. xlvi. 909. [2] *Cf.* vit. Sev. p. 26. [3] διαθήκη.

memory, who was called 'Eleonos,'[1] who was living at that time his heir, because he knew that the man had spent all his property on the poor, ordering that what was left by him also should be distributed to the needy in an exactly similar manner: and Isaiah was to have charge of the distribution of it, who was then educating the sons of the magnificent Eusebius, who were being brought up in the monastic fashion. And the man who made these provisions at the actual very gate of departure from the world named Isaiah 'presbyter,' thereby leaving a written confutation of the dead calumny. For, if he had had the intention
p. 249. of ordaining him bishop after the will,[2] he would not yesterday have named a man in writing 'presbyter,' whom to-morrow he was going to make an unrecorded and unnamed bishop. This is manifestly foolishness. But let the reproof be turned against the head of those who invented the fraud." They, having heard these things and been delighted at what was said, said to me, "One of us was invited by Isaiah through a certain intermediary to become archbishop of Egypt. However all we Egyptians made answer with one consent, 'We for our part do not inquire into this foolish tale of Isaiah's ordination: but we hold to the canon of the holy and great synod of the three hundred and eighteen fathers, knowing an ordination that is performed by one bishop to be void and illegal.'" To this I made answer and said: "Let

[1] *I.e.* ὁ Ἐλεῶνος (gen.).

[2] διαθήκη.

your devoutnesses know that at a later time also, when Paulinus, being patriarch of the city of the Antiochenes, himself alone at the end of his life ordained Evagrius and appointed him his successor, while the orthodox bishops in the East lawfully ordained Flavian archbishop of the same Antioch, a synod was assembled to deal with this case[1]: in the West in the city of p. 250.
Capua: and in the East at Cæsarea in Palestine: because Siricius, who was then archbishop of Rome, had decided that after the discussion at Capua the task of making a more careful investigation of the actual facts of the case[1] should be transferred to the East, Theophilus, the archbishop of the great city of the Alexandrines, having been invited to preside over those who were assembled: who owing to the overthrow of the heathen temples and of the images in Alexander's city had his time occupied and failed to join in assembly with them. And then the synod of saintly bishops which was assembled at Cæsarea in Palestine reported its decree to the God-loving kings of pious memory, Theodosius, Arcadius, and Honorius, and made it known to them in these words: 'For we have read the letter of our reverend brothers to our reverend brother and bishop[2] Theophilus, and that which was written to ourselves the bishops of the East by the bishops at Capua, and that of the religious Siricius the bishop p. 251.
of Rome, to the effect that before all things we must

[1] ὑπόθεσις.

[2] The Greek must have been συνεπίσκοπον.

look to this point, *i.e.* not to disturb the canon of Nicæa which clearly lays down that it is not permissible for the ordination of a bishop to be performed by one only.[1] There was further inserted in the letter of the religious bishop Siricius a decision also upon the hearing that was to be held: in which was inserted the statement "there must be one bishop of Antioch, he who has been legally and ecclesiastically appointed according to the canon of the Synod of Nicæa"; and which clearly decreed that an ordination performed by one is illegal and not to be accepted. With joy therefore we have received the accurate teaching of bishop Siricius concerning the church canons, and, following this letter, we have decreed that these things be ratified: in that we have given legal and just votes, to the effect that we know one bishop of Antioch only the religious lord Flavian the bishop.'"[2] After I had given vent to these words, the devout old men and
p. 252. Egyptian monks to whom I was speaking added that the advocate of Isaiah's deception who promised them the archbishopric of Egypt used to say that the holy Timothy also, the archbishop of the city of the Alexandrines, was ordained by two bishops only, not by three according to the canon. And it has been shown clearly that Peter also the bishop, he of saintly memory, the apostolic man, who came from Iberia, our father, was present there, and held the gospel over Timothy's sacred head, and made up the number of

[1] Mansi ii. 669.

[2] See Journ. of Theol. St. iii. 433.

three bishops: he having been brought by force to the church by the orthodox people, and dragged from the very bed on which he was still lying as being an old and infirm man. But, while he was being carried along by violence, he in an ineffable manner heard a voice from heaven commanding him not to flee from the sacred service.[1] Whence also he gladly and with much assurance[2] assisted in the ordination. Afterwards, when the institution had been thus legally completed, the whole synod of the God-loving bishops of the Egyptian administrative district after these things acknowledged and considered the saintly Timothy as archbishop: and again, when he was returning after exile to Alexander's city, all the p. 253
bishops of the other districts made union with him through the Encyclical letter and proclaimed him archbishop. How then do those presumptuous and unlearned men presume to compare with those legitimate bishops the illegitimate Isaiah, who was not even carried in the womb at all or conceived like the abortive and imperfect offspring of mothers who bring forth abortions, but by the fact of wishing it only created himself bishop for those silly men? These things I have written not because I wish to upset a thing that is tottering on all sides and contains feebleness in itself, but because I desire none of the statements made about him and discussed in my presence in Egypt to be unknown to your diligences:

[1] *Cf.* Zach. Rh. iv. 1.

[2] πληροφορία.

since this other futility also was, as I heard, being advanced by that deceiver: "Some men, you know, in the churches buy ordinations for gold contrary to the canons. Therefore" (he says) "it is in no way beyond the limits of what is proper for me too to become a bishop contrary to strict canonical rule": and the wretched man is not ashamed of daring to confirm his illegal fiction by a similar illegality. Who when taken in adultery says, "I am not an adulterer because so-and-so
p. 254. also is a murderer," and, "I have not offended against the laws because that man also is an offender"? In the next place, in which of the churches of the orthodox, fellow, is it openly put forward as a law that it is right for some men to be ordained for gold, as you make the fictitious and illegal episcopate into a law, and call sin righteousness? If a man tramples in secret on church ordinances, he will give account to the just Judge, but he will not inflict any stain on the appearance of the holy churches, which is confident in its enjoyment of freedom from blame and reproof in all things. I forbear to say that he even presumed to circulate a fictitious letter as having been written by me, which makes a show of finding fault with the fraud concerning him, and gains the plausibility thence derived, but admits that the mockery of the spurious and pretended episcopate was carried to completion. Isaiah therefore, who has been on all points rejected as illegitimate and unhallowed, and has been cast out as a stinking abomination, is trying to force himself into your distinguished believing metropolis, though there also (speaking under

God's permission) he will not find an entrance. For p. 255.
the proof of your faith and loyalty has even by actual experience been disseminated among all men : and we know well and are confident that you are gloriously minded in the Lord, all you who belong to the revered clergy, who have respected the orthodox faith, and all you magnificent and distinguished *ktetores*, who hold the first place, and all you who fill up the body of the church, and cleave to the sound faith. But I have thought it right and seemly for me and a deed consonant with the ordinances of the Spirit not to commit to silence that which has just come into my thoughts, but to testify beforehand to the delusion of error and mark it beforehand and point it out beforehand, lest, when the divine wrath comes upon those who are led to act in violation of the divine laws, and have become the prey of the devil, I find myself under condemnation for those men's blood. For He that speaks through Ezekiel says, "And thou man, I have given thee as a watchman to them of the house of Israel, and thou shalt hear a word from my mouth. When I shall say to the sinner, 'Thou shalt surely die,' and thou speak not that the impious man may refrain from his way, the wicked man shall die in his wickedness, but his blood will I require at thine hand. But, if for thy part thou forewarn the impious man concerning his way that he may turn from it and he turn not from his way, he shall die in his
impiety, and thou shalt deliver thy soul."[1] In the same p. 256.

[1] Eze. iii. 17–19.

way as Isaiah Gregory also has been convicted, as I have learned, in the great city of Alexander. For he too has been detected, and his guile exposed in the minutes[1] of the records.[2] Therefore, learning these things as you do through this mean letter of mine, if anyone presumes to name Gregory or Isaiah a bishop, or shall reckon as valid the profane ordinations performed by them, and does not reject even the very mention of them as being altogether abominable and unlawful, such a man shall be anathema, and shall be found an alien to the glory and communion of the Father and of the Son and of the Holy Spirit, both in this world, and in the world that is to come. If anyone, despising our exile and the persecution by which we are persecuted for the sake of the orthodox faith, shall reckon the things written as nothing, he shall give account to Him who said to the holy apostles and disciples, "But when they persecute you in this city flee to the other";[3] and again, "He that scorneth me and receiveth not my words hath one that judgeth him; the word that I have spoken it shall judge him in the last day";[4] and again, "If they have persecuted me they will also persecute you";[5] and all the expres-
p. 257. sions that are like and similar to these. For, when men have such an unlawful and unholy disposition, and reduce the great mystery of religion to an absurdity, the sacred scripture commands us not even to give

[1] πρᾶξις. [2] ὑπομνήματα. [3] Mt. x. 23.
[4] John xii. 48. [5] John xv. 20.

them greeting, and not to receive these men in the house or take them under our roof, nor to have any dealings at all with them. "If any man," it says, "cometh unto you, and bringeth not this teaching, receive him not in the house, and say not to him 'Hail!': For he that saith to him 'Hail!', is partaker of his evil deeds."[1] And again Paul the Apostle, "But I beseech you, my brethren, to mark them which cause the divisions and offences contrary to the teaching which we have learned, and avoid them. For such men minister not to our Lord Jesus Christ, but to their belly. And by mild words and blessings they deceive the hearts of the simple." If you observe these things, the words also that the same sacred Paul added to these will assuredly be fit to address to you in praise and approbation: and we will truly say, "For your obedience has reached the ears of all men. I rejoice therefore over you."[2] For with this it is well to conclude what we have to say. *The end.*

[1] 2 J. 10, 11. [2] Ro. xvi. 17–19.

PRINTED BY
NEILL AND COMPANY, LIMITED,
EDINBURGH.

CPSIA information can be obtained
at www.ICGtesting.com
Printed in the USA
LVHW081603151122
733182LV00004B/189